OUR AWAKENING WORLD

ROY EUGENE DAVIS

OUR AWAKENING WORLD

Handbook of Spiritual Practices & Guide to Radiant Living in the New Era

ROY EUGENE DAVIS

CSA PRESS, *Publishers*
Lakemont, Georgia 30552

I salute the supreme teacher, the Truth,
whose nature is bliss, who is the giver
of the highest happiness, who is pure
wisdom, who is beyond all qualities and
infinite like the sky, who is beyond words,
who is one and eternal, pure and still,
who is beyond all change and phenomena
and who is the silent witness to all our
thoughts and emotions—I salute Truth,
the supreme teacher.

—Ancient Vedic Hymn

ABOUT THE AUTHOR

Roy Eugene Davis began his spiritual training with Paramahansa Yogananda in 1950, in Los Angeles, California. He was ordained by his guru in 1952 and has taught in this tradition for over thirty years.

Mr. Davis is the author of more than twenty books, some of which are published in five languages. He is the director of Center for Spiritual Awareness, a New Era enlightenment movement with world headquarters in northeast Georgia and branches in U.S. cities, Europe and West Africa.

A steady travel schedule has taken Mr. Davis to major cities in the United States, as well as to Canada, Brazil, England, Europe, Japan and West Africa. His major emphasis is upon man's certain destiny to spiritually awaken and consciously live in harmony with natural laws.

Transcending sectarian boundaries while honoring all authentic traditions, Roy Eugene Davis encourages sincere seekers to enter into a process of needed self-transformation leading to God-realization.

FOREWORD

The recommended way to use this book is to read the text from the beginning to the end, including the Glossary. Then read it again, carefully and repeatedly over a period of time. It is also recommended that the various principles and practices be applied in order to experience benefits.

In preparing this book I have adhered to the tradition of first setting forth an overview of the nature of Consciousness, followed by an explanation of the way to Self-realization, and concluding with spiritual practices and meditation procedures. This is a manual for daily study, a handbook of instruction in spiritual practices, and a guide to radiant living in the New Era.

The reader will find in these pages the basic teachings which support all enlightenment traditions, and details about the process by which personal insight can be experienced. The seers and sages of ages past ever taught that correct information about the nature of Consciousness and man's destiny should be sought after, and that the dedicated aspirant should then enter into needed disciplines and transformation experiences in order to directly realize the highest truth. The spiritual path is not for the superficial devotee who seeks escape through fantasy; it is rather for those persons who are inwardly resolved to consciously "know the truth" in the present life cycle. To this end this book is offered.

When I met my guru, Paramahansa Yogananda, he said to me, "Look neither to the left nor to the right, but move steadily ahead on the path through devotion, selfless work, and deep meditation." He set the example for me. He further said to me, "Teach as I have taught, work as I have worked. Heal as I have healed. The same God is in you that is in me. What I have done, you should do."

For supporting data while preparing this book, I have referred to the published works of several people whom I honor for their past and present contributions to the welfare of humanity. I have also drawn heavily upon the teachings of my guru line and the remembered teachings of many saints whose names are no longer known. If anything here seems new to the reader it is only because the reader is seeing it for the first time. Truth is grounded in Consciousness and is, therefore, without beginning. This is the *sanatana dharma*, the eternal way of righteousness, the way that ever was and ever will be.

ROY EUGENE DAVIS

Lakemont, Georgia (U.S.A.)
September 29, 1987
(the 287th year of the present
ascending Electric Time Cycle)

CONTENTS

ILLUSTRATIONS

PART ONE

Our
Awakening
World

ONE

The Promise of the Ages

That mankind will be enlightened and the world transformed is the hope of humanity and the promise of the ages.
This aspiration, emerging from the depths of the soul, is the
evidence of events to come and the assurance of fulfillment
of the evolutionary plan for the world process.

Sent forth into manifestation from the heart of the Oversoul, the universe is self-nourishing and self-supporting.
Throughout the entire process there is a dynamic inclination
in the direction of ultimate completion. As conscious men
and women learn to increasingly harmonize with nature's laws,
order and righteousness will increasingly prevail. In our current time cycle, we are witnessing the unveiling of predestined
occurrences which no person or circumstance can prevent.

How do we know this? Why can we be so certain about
the near and distant future of Planet Earth and its inhabitants? We know this at the innermost level of our being, and
we have had the vision confirmed by saints and seers of
various times and cultures. Because we have been part of the
cosmic process from the beginning, we subjectively know
how the universe works. This understanding has, from time
to time, been clearly revealed to certain more fully conscious
people and they have shared their understanding with us
through the spoken and written word.

It would be unrealistic to assert that the Age of Enlightenment is upon us, for it is not. It will not dawn for several

thousand years, for reasons which will be explained in the following chapter. But there is evidence that mass spiritual awakening is now taking place on the planet, and that powerful and transformative forces are becoming increasingly influential, expressing through nature herself and through receptive persons. We are in the early stages of an emerging New Era which marks the end of a former Age and the start of a new one.

Fearful persons, not knowing of the bright future which awaits them, expect the worst, even the end of civilization. During the summer of 1980 many articles appeared in newspapers and magazines around the world, providing a long story under the provocative headline: *Obituary Writers Turn to the Earth!* The contents of those articles challenged all who will live through the decades ahead. More articles followed in diverse publications, each usually accompanied by editorial comments.

In brief, this is what millions of readers learned from the various sources: *If present trends continue, the world in the year 2001 will be far more crowded, more polluted, less stable ecologically, and more vulnerable to disruption than the world in which we now live.* There was more: *Serious stresses involving population resources and environment are clearly visible ahead. Despite greater material output, the world's population will be poorer in many ways than today.*

That was the conclusion stated in a report made to the President of the United States by thirteen government agencies which had taken three years to compile the data. Current trends indicated a growth in world population at a rate of one hundred million annually. The economic gap, it was predicted, would increase between the rich and the poor. World oil production would reach its limits and new energy sources would have to be found before then. Water resources might become erratic as world population doubled and forests diminished. Faulty use of available farmlands might continue. Concentrations of carbon dioxide and ozone-depleting chemicals were expected to increase at rates that could warm the world's climate and possibly result in the melting of the polar ice caps.

Add to this the rising crime rate in many parts of the world, the continuing exploitation of minority groups, the testing and stockpiling of nuclear weapons, the existence of a human-centered educational system, and the proliferation of music and entertainment which undermine social values and encourage immoral behavior, and one may indeed wonder about the world's future.

I wish, as do many, that I had immediate solutions to all of these problems and that the solutions could be implemented immediately. But there is *something* that is the solution: it is the force of evolution, the trend in the direction of ordered growth and unfoldment. The innate supporting influence of the life process will insure that every major obstacle to the completion of divine purposes will be removed, as creative solutions emerge in the minds of responsive individuals and are taken to heart by those who can act upon them.

What many in our world do not know is that a higher intelligence is responsible for ultimate ends. I do not minimize the challenges before us. I do, however, want to share a message of hope and to include suggestions of a practical nature. An attitude of despair often pervades social consciousness when dire predictions are aired, because the average person feels himself to be incapable of being effectively useful in the face of such odds. A popular tool used by some fundamentalist religious leaders has been that of pointing to the possibility of near-future global catastrophe as an indication that mankind's future is about to be curtailed, and that therefore the time for religious conversion is at hand. In a sense they are right, but I doubt that any of them know the true larger picture. Even among those in the frontlines of what is believed to be the humanity enlightenment movement, few are fully aware of the grand cosmic process now unfolding. Their vision is often faulty and their lives seldom grounded in God-realization.

Much literature has been published in recent years predicting the worst, and the best. Some write of coming disaster, while others write in glowing terms of the Golden Age that is just around the corner, perhaps as soon as the turn of the century. Some who profess to have psychic abilities often make foolish predictions and others, who see the opportunity to profit from the anxieties and fears of people, offer invitations to the "chosen" to gather together to form "safe" communities. The world is doomed, they preach, but "we" will be saved and begin again. Hypnotic subjects, or those acting the part, claim to channel guidance from "masters" who dwell in rarified spiritual realms. Thus do immaturity and charlatanism walk hand in hand.

Every now and again the call goes forth for the faithful to gather, to meditate, sing, hug and rejoice, to acknowledge a "turning point" during which high frequency energies will flood the earth with redeeming force. The signs are all about us to see, the evidence of world transformation is at hand, but few seem to take the evidence seriously and to follow through with the program of personal self-transformation and responsible behavior which alone can enable them to become mature citizens of the New Era. Of course, millions are already doing their best in a quiet way, and they go unnoticed, which is probably the most useful way to go.

The Years Ahead: Time of Challenge and of Opportunity

What more challenging opportunity for personal growth and world service could we have than the one before us? This is surely the time to gather our inner forces and rise to the occasion. Divine forces will be aroused in us and heretofore undreamed of abilities will come to the fore. Others will be inspired and the forces of nature will work with us in constructive ways.

My guru, Paramahansa Yogananda, once spoke about world transformation to a group of disciples, of which I was one. He said, "God's will will be done, no matter whether random individuals participate in the process or not. But how much better it is for us to participate, in harmony with His will!" He referred to the fact that when we surrender to the process and go along with it, we are carried along as conscious participants.

It is not possible to confront present challenges in parts, for the confrontation must be total. To work to eliminate hunger, for example, without solving the problem of pollution of the environment, would prove futile in the final outcome. To stabilize the economies of nations and discover new energy resources will be necessary, but even if man's needs are met, and they will be, without global intellectual and spiritual awakening the planet will not truly reflect the New Era. A secure human existence would be welcomed for a while, but we would soon discover that even with every material thing at hand, something was still missing. Along with assuring the health of the planet and the wellness of society, there is the need to ensure an enlightened society. This requires spiritual education, not merely emphasis upon social and political stability.

Let us, from now forward, encourage our family, friends and associates to deepen their spiritual lives, to acquire the necessary education, and to fulfill their responsibilities with conscious attention and utmost skill. Let us neutralize the negativity which contributes to unfounded fears and anxiety. Let us spread the word that there is an intelligently directed power supporting the universe and that man can learn to cooperate with it. Let us know that the intelligence behind the power has a plan and a purpose for the currently unfolding world process and for all who share in it. Let us believe, with pure faith, that hunger, war, crime and all major challenges soon will no longer mar planetary consciousness.

An important ingredient in the now unfolding planetary transformation process is for individuals, groups and nations to accept the ideal of world harmony and to cooperate in all practical ways to assist in orderly change. A person who thinks in terms of a material universe cannot comprehend that a universal intelligence is intimately involved in human affairs. Life is one organic whole. One Consciousness appears in almost infinite expression, and remains one Consciousness.

Some refer to It as Life, the Oversoul, or God. The names are many, but the Reality is one.

Those of limited understanding may try to tell us that man turns to God because he cannot handle his personal circumstances. This is often true, and if one sincerely turns to the source, one will discover an inner strength that before was absent. There are those who assert that faith in God is but psychological support for a mind lacking the power of will. Seers tell us differently. They inform us of the true nature of the universal process and they explain how it is directed by a primal intelligence. They inform us that life is naturally inclined in the direction of unfoldment, creative expression, and completion. They educate us to the fact that a support system is innate to nature, which nourishes it and sustains it when allowed to do so.

As the years unfold we will experience increasing evidence that we are moving into a New Era. Such evidence has been before us for the past century but not all have discerned it. From now onward, changes will occur with such rapidity that anyone who is the least bit conscious cannot fail to recognize them. There is no need to fight with those who may persist, for a duration, in their Dark Age ways. The master key is to give attention and energy to all that is worthwhile; that which is not useful in the New Age will fade away. All beliefs, behavior, plans and efforts which cannot harmonize with near and future destined unfoldments will be discarded. Some people who are resistant to change will have to stand aside and watch the rest of the world move on to its destined fulfillment.

What are the solutions to currently known problems, and and ones which may unfold in the future? Are there answers to meet every need? Is it possible that a higher influence will intervene?

Every problem has a solution, every proper question has an answer, and, yes, a higher influence is now intervening to ensure orderly transformation. The infusion of supernatural power manifests for the purpose of continuing the process of growth and unfoldment. This is well stated in the Bhagavad Gita (4:6, 7):

Whenever and wherever divinity becomes subdued and humanity struggles to emerge out of ignorance, then and there I incarnate myself. To assure salvation to the virtuous, to awaken the ignorant, and thereby to manifest divinity on earth, I incarnate myself from time to time.

Thus is the *avatara* influence made manifest on earth. The "descent of light and power" is a matter of superior influences, with origins in the Godhead, moving into cosmic and planetary affairs. To overly personalize the process is to attempt to focus the influence through one or more personalities and to miss the point of what occurs. True, from time to time, illumined souls are born into the world with a special mission, and they are often recognized because they embody all of the divine qualities we associate with a pure and conscious life. But God is never the personality-person—God is the presence and reality expressing through the personality. To frantically look for the coming of a savior who will set conditions right and restore the world to its ideal place can often result in our failure to unfold the divine capacities we have within us.

The avatara influence works in impersonal ways, also. It works to stir the sleeping soul forces of the masses and to ensure the balance of nature. In this way the divine nature of all people begins to come to the surface and fine energies influence the mental field of the planet, as well as the collective consciousness of humanity. When the mental field of the planet is thus influenced, changes in the direction of more harmonious planetary conditions begin to occur. Even weather patterns can be changed and nature herself can become increasingly supportive. Scientists experience useful breakthroughs. Persons engaged in research discover new ways to do things. Persons of influence in business and politics are able to solve problems more effectively. Religious leaders become more God-realized and are able to share their realizations with their people. Life knows how to take care of essential matters when needs are present.

Because of prevailing divine influences I do not fear the future, nor should you. Souls newly awakening will, as they persist with right resolve, be led into the paths appropriate to them. The intelligence of God knows how to see to the needs of every person in just the right way. The reality of God surrounds us, pervades us and is specialized *as* us. Man is not a material being; he is a blend of Spirit and matter and is in the world as an integral part of the process of creation. God is the Life, the Being, the Power, and the Substance making everything possible.

Let us examine a few matters which will always need to be addressed so long as we are involved with material creation. Remember, as we do this, that matter is really Consciousness, appearing *as* matter, and that subtle influences cause matter and material circumstances to change.

Human beings require shelter, food, resources to allow them to function freely, and a feeling of well-being. The resources to meet all basic needs are already at hand. There is an abundance of everything to provide shelter, food and economic freedom to every man, woman and child on the planet—right now. All that is needed is the willingness on the part of responsible and capable people to see to fair distribution, and education to provide people with the knowledge of how to be self-responsible. There can be no excuse for not seeing to the basic needs of all of the people on the planet. Groundless excuses may be given for not doing this, but there can be no valid excuse. Before long, attention will be taken from competitive and destructive involvements and focused upon matters which are important. This should occur over the next few decades.

By observing trends, and by knowing inner causes responsible for outer effects, it is possible to see into the future and predict with accuracy what is to unfold in the years ahead. Let us look into the future, together, and view the world our children and grandchildren will experience. You, too, may see many of these things in embryonic form, before you move on to the subtle realms.

As soon as it is clearly realized that abundant resources

exist, and competition no longer rules the marketplace, wars and rumors of wars will end. Fossil fuels will be replaced by energy converted from solar rays and by the utilization of nature's forces, forces which can never be depleted and will not pollute the earth's atmosphere.

Religious, racial and cultural differences will dissolve as individuals become increasingly aware of their innate divinity. It will be universally understood that we are rays of the same light and that we share a common destiny. Differences will exist, contributing to variety without detracting from social harmony and unity of purpose. Instead of churches where different creeds are taught, temples will serve the spiritual needs of people and meditation centers will be gathering places for the devout, who will there enjoy communion with God; from such places beneficial radiations will flow into the collective consciousness of the race.

With the permanent solving of survival-related problems, people will be free to pursue creative ventures, to study the arts and sciences, and to further explore the nature of Consciousness. Disease will diminish and healthy, long life will be normal. With understanding will come maturity and, with maturity, will come complete harmony with nature's laws.

The ideal life is being experienced now by all who are possessed of a New Era consciousness, for it is out of our consciousness, and our mental states, that our life experiences unfold. This is why the major emphasis must be upon spiritual education for the purpose of informing the planet's population of the true origin, nature and destiny of man. Unenlightened people cannot be citizens of the New Era. By its very character it will require intelligence and surrendered cooperation with the forces which make it possible.

How marvelous is the cosmos, God's intricate creation! How marvelous is man, a part of the process yet destined to transcend it! The life force that permeates the universe floods our being with enlivening influence, and the consciousness of the atom is our own. We are witnessing the unfoldment of divine capacities and the emergence of the long-envisioned New Era. Rejoice!

TWO

Cycles of World Destiny
and Our Emerging New Era

It is unfortunate that millions of people have continued to believe that the world is presently in the Dark Age, the time phase known as *Kali Yuga*. On the contrary, we are presently in the dawning of an ascending cycle, an emerging New Era, which will carry us, some thousands of years from now, to the peak of the next Golden Age, an era of world enlightenment and fulfillment.

The history of Planet Earth can be traced with a fair degree of accuracy by closely examining the phases through which we have passed, when these phases can be dated. Folklore and philosophical speculation can be suspect, but when historical incidents are found to be recorded in relationship to astronomical configurations we can more accurately place them in the stream of time.

The reasons for the misconception shared by many is that, heretofore, accurate knowledge has not generally been available, and even those who have had access to it were not always able to comprehend its significance. Too, many "teachers" who are held in high regard by their followers likewise persist in asserting the Dark Age myth, either because they do not know any better or because it satisfies the emotional needs of those who hear it. Now, with the rapid acceleration of spiritual awakening on the planet, the time has come to more widely disseminate the good news about our awakening world, and about mankind's future in it.

The unenlightened mind does not like to be challenged by facts which threaten its seemingly stable condition, based as it often is on lack of knowledge and incorrect data. However, the Self-realization path is for the spiritual warrior, not for the weak or timid, nor for those who are double-minded and desirous of thinking one way while engaged in a futile attempt to live another.

In an ancient Sanskrit scripture, the *Manu Samhita*, we read:

> Four thousand years, they say, is the Golden Age of the world. Its morning twilight has just as many hundreds, and its period of evening dusk is the same length. In the other three Ages, with their morning and evening twilights, the thousands and hundreds decrease by one. That fourfold cycle comprising 12,000 years is called an Age of the gods.

The cycles referred to in this scripture are related to the precession of the equinoxes, the slight increase in distance of the equinoctial points in reference to a fixed star, which is taken as Aries 0 degrees in the zodiac of the constellations. The ancients believed this star to be Alcyone, the brightest star of the Pleiades, one of several of that star cluster, and around which our sun moves, taking with it its planets.

Our solar system is near the outer edge of the Milky Way galaxy, which is believed to be hundreds of millions of light years across. Billions of suns exist in the Milky Way galaxy, many of them far larger than our own. The other galaxies in space are without number, and are separated from our own by trillions of light years.

The Babylonians referred to the fixed star Alcyone as "the foundation stone." The Arabs named it "the immortal seal or type" and "the central one." Vedic astronomers referred to it as "the mother," and the Greek word Alcyone signifies "peace." There is an interesting verse in the Old Testament

(Job 38:31): "Canst thou bind the sweet influences of Pleiades, or loose the bands of Orion?"

The information here shared was first published in 1894, in a small book titled *The Holy Science*, written by Sri Yukteswar, guru of Paramahansa Yogananda. After years of deep study and contemplation, Sri Yukteswar concluded that the 24,000-year cycle, the time it takes for the sun to return to its place, calculated as Aries 0, corresponded to the Ages referred to in the Manu Samhita, with four descending Ages occurring during a 12,000-year period and another four ascending Ages occurring during the following 12,000 years. There have been different opinions about the actual time it takes for a complete cycle of the precession of the equinoxes to occur, but Vedic astronomers believe that 24,000 years is correct, making allowances for the fact that the movement varies in speed from time to time.

Moons revolve around planets and planets revolve around the sun. The sun moves in its orbit, with its planets, and all participate in the interchange of universal energies. According to Vedic sources, our sun in its orbit moves toward, and away from, a "center of creative power" which contributes to the unveiling of intelligence in man, or to its covering, depending upon whether Planet Earth is near it or more distant from it. During the time phase when intelligence is unveiled, man as a whole is enlightened, and this reflects in society as a Golden Age. During the time phase when intelligence is dimmed, the majority of people on the planet are restricted to material consciousness and this condition reflects in society as a Dark Age. In between are periods of various degrees of awareness, reflecting in society as corresponding Ages.

The creative power source referred to above is known as *Vishnunabhi*, the Navel of Vishnu. Vishnu is the aspect of the Godhead involved with creation which is responsible for the preservation of the world. Sri Yukteswar referred to the creative power source as Universal Magnetism, which acts upon all life, using celestial bodies as distribution points through which energies are channeled. In this way it regulates the mental characteristics of man.

Each of these 12,000-year periods brings about a complete change in the mental condition of the majority of people on the planet. There are always some rare souls who are so highly realized that they are not influenced by external forces. They remain the custodians of wisdom and sometimes function as teachers of the race. The complete 24,000-year cycle is called an *Electric Time Cycle.*

Starting for the purpose of reckoning from the bottom of the Time Cycle, during the time phase of the most widespread inertia, the true Dark Age prevails. A Dark Age cycle is 1,200 years in duration, calculating 1,000 years as the duration of the Age itself, plus 200 years before and after as mutation phases, the merging of one cycle into another. This represents 1/20th of the sun's grand orbit. The mental ability of the average person during this cycle is but one-fourth unfolded, so that man cannot grasp anything but the most obvious external matters. He is then in material consciousness, able to perceive only the objective environment. Intuition is not awakened, and intellectual powers are for the most part absent.

The second period of 2,400 years of the ascending cycle, when the sun moves through 2/20ths of its orbit, is called the Electric Age because, during this period of time, human intellect begins to comprehend the fine forces in nature, the electricities and their attributes, and the fields of magnetism, which are the creating principles of the external world. This is the time cycle in which we now live, rather than in the Dark Age, as some still believe. The last Dark Age concluded around the year A.D. 1700 and, as of this writing (1987), we are 187 years into the ascending Electrical Cycle, almost totally removed from the influences of the preceding cycle. This is why we are observing such a quickening of consciousness and intellectual capacities among the people of the planet. History confirms that, with the emergence of the current cycle almost two hundred years ago, in the West man began to discover and make use of electricity and other fine matters. Now, the fields of magnetism are being researched and their understanding applied in practical ways. Our present

CHART OF ELECTRIC TIME CYCLES

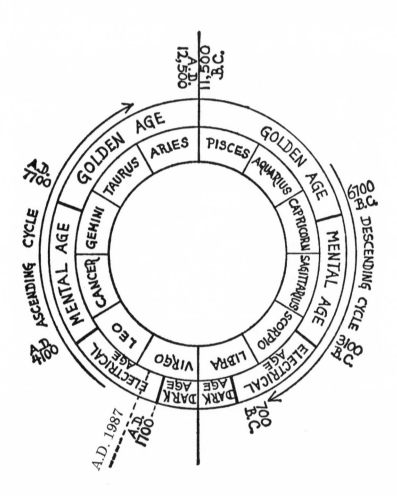

time cycle will continue until A.D. 4100, bringing with it astounding advances in science and vast improvements in all matters relating to the well-being of Earth's inhabitants.

The third ascending period of 3,600 years, during which the sun passes through 3/20ths of its orbit, is called the Mental Age, because the human intellect is then able to grasp the *source* of electric forces upon which creation is based, as well as the existence and nature of cosmic mind. Telepathy will then be the norm and man will almost fully harness the forces of nature in wise and benevolent ways.

The remaining fourth period, during which the sun passes through 4/20ths of its orbit, is called the Enlightenment Age, the true Golden Age of man. During this Age the human intellect can easily grasp the true nature of Consciousness, That from which the worlds have emerged. This period will last 4,800 years and then merge into another period of like length before the process of descent begins and continues in reverse order, until another Dark Age occurs.

The Golden Age is almost ten thousand years in duration, with the other Ages shorter and the Dark Age comprising two phases of 1,200 years each; they, like their opposite, the Golden Age, span two consecutive occurrences. Because of the force of evolution, the force of ordered development, each succeeding Dark Age is less dark than the one preceding it, so that with continuing grand cycles of 24,000 years, the whole of mankind manifests progressive spiritual maturity.

Civilizations rise and fall because of the electric influences by which all of nature is ruled. Souls incarnate during Ages when their personal needs and karmic conditions can best be met and worked with. In this way, because of the law of correspondences (as within, so without), souls flow to circumstances most opportune for their learning and unfoldment.

The period around A.D. 500 was the darkest part of the last Dark Age. From that point the sun again began its move in the direction of the creative force center and the intellectual capacities of man began to be unveiled. It was not until around A.D. 1700 that positive indications of man's growing perceptive abilities began to be acknowledged as a result of

his discoveries of some of nature's properties, coinciding with
the end of the last Dark Age and heralding the onset of the
current Electric Age.

Among the general population today are represented the
various stages through which mankind moves. We have among
us many who are still influenced by Dark Age mentality and
who are aware only of their immediate material surroundings.
Then we have those who understand, to a degree, the properties of electricity and magnetism, those who are capable of
consciously comprehending the nature of cosmic mind, and a
few who are fully awake and God-conscious. Persons who can
only comprehend in limited fashion must look to those who
are more conscious for instruction and guidance. More conscious individuals should continue their quest for knowledge
and increased realization, while assisting others who are less
aware in the best way that they can.

As we increasingly understand the workings of Consciousness through nature, we see that there is indeed an intelligence
which is responsible for the destiny of man and his world.
Many historians have incorrectly blamed man for past major
catastrophes because they were not able to understand the
true inner causes of outer effects, the subtle influences which
determine occurrences on the gross outer level.

Seers who have studied the phenomenon of cycles say
that every 6,000 years mankind undergoes a minor dramatic
change in the course of evolution, and every 12,000 years a
major change. We are now moving through one of the major
periods of transformation. This does not mark a period of
disaster, however; it evidences one of man's internal transfor-
mations and, thus, exercises profound constructive effects on
the global scene.

Legend has it that the fall of Atlantis, presumed by some
to be a mere myth, began around 11,500 B.C. just after the
beginning of the decline of the last Golden Age. Plato, in the
Critias, described the Golden Age condition of Atlantis. It
was a philosophic democracy in which the arts flourished and
the sciences were cultivated in great universities. Man had no
enemies and war was unknown. Gradually, because of less-

ening influences from the creative power center, men began to lose their spiritual awareness and with this their virtues. Personal ambition and corruption ensued and nature's forces ran rampant. Atlantis was devastated by cataclysmic earthquakes around 10,184 B.C., approximately 1,316 years after the Golden Age began to dim.

Some minor prophets would have us believe that civilization declined because of man's evil ways. While it is true that short-term effects can, and often do, result from man's unwise behavior, major effects are due to deeper causes in which man is but a participant. The light of Atlantis lingered on, because poets and philosophers preserved the story through transmitted oral tradition. The minor "glory" of later civilizations preceding the Dark Age represented but the dying embers of a once great Age of world enlightenment.

Not every transition of Ages is marked by dramatic outer change. Often transitions occur gradually, leaving historians no inkling of the causes for such changes in the behavior of men. While changes are occurring during our present time phase, we need not overly anticipate any major disasters to the planet or any global wars. A "thorough cleansing" of the planet is not required for the emergence of the Era now unfolding, prophets of doom to the contrary. Therefore, do not believe those who would attempt to frighten you with dire predictions. They but speak from ignorance and know not of what they speak, or why.

Why Many Wrongly Believe the Dark Age Yet Prevails

Many readers may be interested in knowing Sri Yukteswar's conclusions as to why some people are of the mistaken opinion that the world is still in the Dark Age. After long investigation, Sri Yukteswar discovered the reason for this error.

Some sources claim that the Dark Age will continue for another 432,000 years, truly a gloomy prospect! This error was made in India about 700 B.C. during the reign of Raja Parikshit. Prior to that time Maharaja Yudhisthira, noticing evidence of the coming Dark Age, turned his throne over to his grandson and retired to the seclusion of the Himalayan mountains, taking with him his astronomers and astrologers, and leaving no one in the remaining court who could correctly calculate the movements of the celestial bodies. The astronomers did not want to record the coming of the Dark Age because they did not want to create fear in the minds of the people, and they recorded the beginning of the Dark Age as the beginning of the following Electric Age. They wanted the public to believe they were moving in an upward cycle instead of into a downward one. About A.D. 499 the mistake in the almanac was discovered, but not the reason for it. The almanac recorded the length of the Dark Age as one period of 1,200 years, instead of two periods (1,200 descending and 1,200 ascending). The later astrologers assumed that the Dark Age years were not real solar years but rather "years of the gods," with one year being a day and 1,200 years amounting to 432,000 solar years. When this information is explained, even today, many refuse to accept it, either because they cannot understand the calculations or because they prefer to remain with traditional opinion. An unfortunate result of this false teaching regarding the status of our present time cycle is that it serves to create a mood of pessimism among those who hear and believe it.

Vedic scriptures place the world-age within a Kali Yuga, or Dark Age, in relationship to a much longer universal cycle. The universal cycle is said to be 4,300,560,000 years in duration. This is calculated by finding the relationship between the length of the solar year and a multiple of *pi* (3.1416, the ratio of the circumference to the diameter of a circle). The life span of the whole universe is calculated at 314,159,000, 000,000 (three hundred and fourteen trillion, one hundred fifty-nine billion) solar years. The universe is currently considered to be about fifteen billion years old, leaving most of the years in the universal cycle remaining for life processes to continue. This total duration of manifest creation is referred to as a "Day of Brahma," the duration of outward manifestation, after which creation is drawn back into the field of God for a like duration of rest.

Our Present Time Phase
and "The Hour of God"

The years of the twentieth century spanning the ninth decade have been referred to by various seers as the period in which "the hour of God" would occur. By this is meant the critical point reached when, because of mankind's moving into the ascending cycle during the last several years and marking our withdrawal from the effects of the Dark Age would be experienced and humanity would collectively understand the necessity of cultivating the virtues and deepening the spiritual life. As I write these pages we are moving through this time phase; the "hour of God" is being experienced now.

Communications technology almost instantly brings news of events distant from us to our homes via the medium of television. We are being made increasingly aware of trends and happenings which confirm the need for personal and collective responsible behavior. Many are overloaded with information, and bewildered by it. They often feel that present challenges are of such magnitude that as individuals they are helpless in the face of them.

This is an opportunity for growth, an opportunity to rise from small, limited ways of thinking and to actualize inborn capacities. The only way for one to be prepared for the New Era is to be spiritually mature. The remainder of this book is dedicated to providing information about the nature of Consciousness and ways to enable the reader to experience the full unfoldment of soul qualities, in line with his present aptitude and inner aspiration.

PART TWO

One
Life, Being,
Power &
Substance

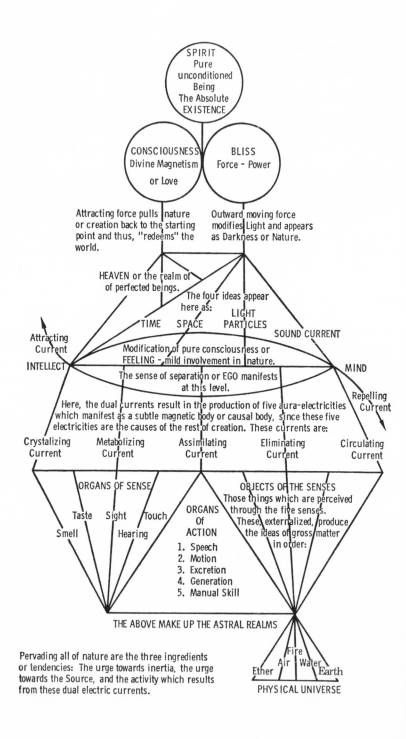

SPIRIT
Pure
unconditioned
Being
The Absolute
EXISTENCE

CONSCIOUSNESS
Divine Magnetism
or Love

BLISS
Force - Power

Attracting force pulls nature
or creation back to the starting
point and thus, "redeems" the
world.

Outward moving force
modifies Light and appears
as Darkness or Nature.

HEAVEN or the realm of
of perfected beings.

The four ideas appear
here as:

TIME   SPACE   LIGHT
PARTICLES

SOUND CURRENT

Attracting
Current

INTELLECT

Modification of pure consciousness or
FEELING – mild involvement in nature.

The sense of separation or EGO manifests
at this level.

MIND

Repelling
Current

Here, the dual currents result in the production of five aura-electricities
which manifest as a subtle magnetic body or causal body, since these five
electricities are the causes of the rest of creation. These currents are:

Crystalizing
Current

Metabolizing
Current

Assimilating
Current

Eliminating
Current

Circulating
Current

ORGANS OF SENSE

Taste   Sight   Touch

Smell   Hearing

ORGANS
Of
ACTION

1. Speech
2. Motion
3. Excretion
4. Generation
5. Manual Skill

OBJECTS OF THE SENSES
Those things which are perceived
through the five senses.
These, externalized, produce
the ideas of gross matter
in order:

THE ABOVE MAKE UP THE ASTRAL REALMS

Pervading all of nature are the three ingredients
or tendencies: The urge towards inertia, the urge
towards the Source, and the activity which results
from these dual electric currents.

Fire
Air   Water
Ether   Earth

PHYSICAL UNIVERSE

The Twenty-five Categories of Cosmic Manifestation

One Life, Being, Power and Substance is responsible for the manifestation, maintenance and transformation of nature. This essence and reality is called by various names by people of the world. One term commonly used is *Consciousness*, as self-aware, self-existent and self-functioning. Consciousness requires no object for its existence for it is the knower, the act of knowing and the known, simultaneously. While Consciousness can be known *about* as a result of objective and subjective analysis, it can be fully comprehended only when experienced.

When we perceive through our senses we are limited, because our senses convey and reveal to the mind only a small portion of the universe which is present and available at any given moment. For instance, it is estimated that, when using our senses alone, we are able to perceive but a billionth of the totality of electromagnetic waves and other forces in nature. Aided by sense-extenders such as telescopes, microscopes and other man-devised instruments, we are able to perceive radio waves below the color red in the spectrum and gamma rays and X-rays in the electromagnetic spectrum above the color violet. There exists beyond these ranges a vast universe of pulsating forces to which we presently do not have normal access. Seers inform us, however, that it is possible to turn within, take leave of the senses, and thus actually become aware of the subtle and fine forces of nature. It is in this way that one is able to understand the inner workings of nature upon which all outer manifestation depends.

There is another reason why we are not usually able to see clearly what is presently at hand. We have grown accustomed to our present world view, our present way of looking at the world, and because we are not used to seeing phenomena which have not been common to our experience we literally do not see what is before us. Even what is obvious to several members of a group will be reported differently, depending upon who is telling his version. Some people cannot comprehend the existence of God, much less understand the true nature of God. Others cannot comprehend the possibility of living an ordered, successful life, because they see only disorder and, to them, obvious choices of varying degrees of failure. Some cannot believe in the existence of miracles, occurrences which, although unusual, are nonetheless due to the actions of subtle natural laws. Others cannot believe even when they see a miracle, because it is not part of their mindset; because they have never before seen a miracle, for them it is beyond belief.

To clearly comprehend the truth, the totality of Consciousness from fine, to subtle, to gross expressions, we must be willing to occasionally transcend sense- and mind-identification and examine the nature of Consciousness from the level of soul awareness. In this way we can directly see and truly know, often in a flash of insight, an illuminating flash of revelation, during which everything is obvious beyond a shadow of a doubt.

The soul, being a specialized unit of pure consciousness, possesses innate knowledge of the One Life, Being, Power and Substance. This is why we state that "knowledge is grounded in consciousness." Consciousness is self-complete, so knowledge of it is innate to it.

Centuries ago, sages contemplated the nature of Consciousness and discovered the why and the how of creation, the purpose for it, and the subtle self-interactions which occur throughout the universe; they also discovered how souls might awaken from involuntary identification with matter. This understanding they shared with receptive persons, disciples on the enlightenment path who were suitable for training and instruction.

To these sages were revealed twenty-five categories of cosmic manifestation, from the initial impulse to express to the state of full material manifestation. The explanation given in enumerating these categories comprises the Vedic philosophical system known as *Samkhya*. The twenty-five categories provide an explanation of how the universe unfolded, from the initial impulse through to full manifestation, and the movements and rhythms involved in maintaining, transforming and dissolving the universe. Further, explanations are given for the purpose of enabling the aspirant to understand the process of soul awakening and final liberation of consciousness.

The One Life expresses as all variations of life throughout the universe, from the Godhead to the physical worlds. One Being is the beingness, the inner reality, of all life units and life forms. One Power expresses as all variations of force and energy in creation. One Substance manifests as all aspects of nature and as all forms in nature. One Thing, Consciousness, through a process of self-involvement, is enacting the cosmic drama. Therefore, where you are, where I am, the all-ness of Consciousness is; it has only to be discerned. It is not far removed, nor do we have to think that it will take years to "reach the goal" of Self-realization. All the truth there is, is presently available for us to be known. All the freedom there is, is now available to be experienced. Whatever is required by us to fulfill our duties and accomplish our worthy purposes is at hand, awaiting our recognition and acceptance.

As you study this theme, do not despair if you are not able to at once clearly understand it in its entirety. Continue to live a dedicated, purposeful life. Continue to meditate and study. Continue to contemplate the nature of Consciousness. You will surely mature and unfold, until you discover that you are increasingly capable, increasingly insightful, and increasingly aware of the vibrant and radiant reality of God at all times. Readers who come from diverse religious traditions will better understand their chosen sacred scriptures as a result of understanding even a portion of what is here shared. Regardless of his station in society or his vocation, the discerning student of this divine science will find that he is able to fulfill life's purposes more comfortably and graciously as a result of his increasing understanding.

The Unmanifest Field
of Pure Consciousness (1)

The absolute, transcendental reality underlying everything, even the finest level of creation, is itself devoid of characteristics, attributes or modifications, but contains within itself limitless possibilities. It is the source of everything, the realm of pure being, yet it is removed from creation in that it is not influenced or affected by anything that occurs in creation. It causes everything to be, but itself is not acted upon. It contains all latent possibilities and is all-pervasive. Man can experience it by turning inward, during thoughtless superconscious meditation. The unmanifest field of pure consciousness cannot be described, but it can be known through experience.

In the Bhagavad Gita (10:8—11) we read:

I am the origin of all, everything proceeds from Me. Thinking thus, the wise filled with the sentiment of devotion devote themselves to Me. Their minds absorbed in Me, their pranas entering into Me, enlightening each other, narrating about Me, they are ever satisfied and ever delighted. To them who are ever joined in yoga and devote themselves with pleasure and love, I confer the yoga of wisdom whereby they come close to Me. Dwelling in their inner Self, to favor them, out of compassion I destroy their darkness born of ignorance with the brilliant lamp of knowledge.

During deep meditation, when awareness transcends feelings and thoughts, one experiences pure consciousness, that "one without a second," that reality which needs no object to support it. It is by such repeated experience that the soul is eventually redeemed, even while embodied. The cleansing light of pure consciousness shines into the mind and body, removing everything unlike itself, until the organism is restructured and all restricting characteristics are dissolved.

The Godhead: Only Manifest Being (2)

The Godhead is the initial, and only, outer expression of the unmanifest field of consciousness. From the Godhead the worlds are produced, and by it they are maintained.

The origin of the word *God* can be traced via the Germanic languages to the Indo-European, in which a corresponding ancestor form of the word means "invoked one." The non-Germanic origin is the Sanskrit *hu*, meaning "invoke the gods." This is found in the Rig Veda, the oldest known scripture of which we have present knowledge.

Unlike the unmanifest field of pure consciousness, in the field of God there are attributes; the Godhead can therefore be conceptualized, examined, experienced and explained. However, the totality of God can never be fully described, any more than the totality of the universe can be fully described, because movement and change are ever taking place within the Godhead and within the universe.

Our concepts about God can help us in our devotional inquiry, but concepts will eventually necessarily give way to knowledge. One can think of God as the omnipotent creator, as father, as friend, even as mother (when expressed as nature), but all ideas about God will dissolve as one truly experiences the reality of God.

In the Godhead, three attributes prevail at all times. These, in Sanskrit, are known as *sattva, rajas,* and *tamas guna.* The word *guna* means "that which contains," and the gunas are the attributes in the Godhead, and throughout nature, which influence. Sattva guna is purity, brightness, the attribute nearest to pure existence. Rajas guna is dynamic, in motion, causing change. Tamas guna is heavy, dulling, and causes inertia.

Tamas guna results in gross manifestation, rajas guna results in activity and motion in the worlds, and sattva guna returns nature to the field of God. Tamas guna manifests, rajas guna causes movement and transformation, and sattva guna results in equilibrium and balance. Even sattva guna will be transcended by the devotee when pure consciousness is experienced. During transcendental consciousness there is no influence of nature upon the soul. There is only the experience of existence. Without mental modifications, without objective awareness, the soul rests in the awareness of being.

Movement in the Direction
of Material Manifestation (3)

When the three gunas, the attributes, are in perfect balance the Godhead is self-contained and the universe is non-existent. When the gunas stir and tamas guna prevails the process of world manifestation begins.

From the Bhagavad Gita (8:16—19) the words of Krishna:

All the way to the realm of Brahma, the Godhead, all the worlds revolve again and again. Upon reaching Me, there is no more rebirth. People who know day and night know that the day of Brahma (God as creator) extends to a thousand aeons also. All the manifest entities arise from the unmanifest upon the coming of day and upon the coming of the night they dissolve into that very thing called the unmanifest. The aggregate of beings and elements, born again and again, is then dissolved at the coming of the night, quite helplessly, and is produced again upon the arrival of the day.

Philosophical speculation has it that a "day" of creation lasts four billion, three hundred and twenty-six million solar years, as we calculate time on Planet Earth. It is assumed that an equal "duration" of non-time is the occasion of non-manifestation, when creation is drawn back into the field of God.

Paramahansa Yogananda once told me that many saints "are content" to experience the joy and bliss of God-communion for millions of years, remaining this side of full absorption in the unmanifest field. These would also be souls which might again become involved with a new creation after a duration of non-manifestation and the beginning of a new "day" of manifestation.

The initial outward flow of force from the Godhead is referred to, in Eastern scriptures, as the *word*, the primal sound current (Om, Aum). It possesses the characteristics of force when it is flowing outward, and of attraction when it is attuned with sattva guna. It carries subtle-element characteristics into manifestation and it can be communed with to flow attention back to the source during meditation. It is that from which all varied forces in the universe emanate and that into which all forces dissolve.

When the meditator merges his consciousness in the sound current he feels himself to be one with it. If his urge is to flow to the source of sound he can follow it to the field of God and then experience pure consciousness. By resting in the awareness of the sound current, whatever he needs or wants is sure to manifest in his world in a natural and spontaneous manner.

The Primal Urge to Express;
Individualization and Self-
Involvement of Consciousness (3, 4)

In The Gospel According to Saint John (1:1—3) we find a reference to the process of manifestation:

> In the beginning was the Word, and the Word was with God, and the Word was God. The same was in the beginning with God. All things were made by him; and without him was not anything made that was made.

The creative force, the word, imbued with intelligence, is the "self-begotten" of God. Everything else is an expression of this creative force. As the creative force flows it acts upon itself to express as the forces and aspects of nature. The aspects are: the creative force itself; fine particles which form atoms; space, as the medium in which events occur; and time, making possible duration. Taken together, these comprise the primal substance of which all things are formed.

Creation, while illusory, is not an illusion. It is Consciousness-manifesting-as nature. Unawakened man, not knowing the inner side of nature, perceives only the outer side of nature and assumes the outer to alone be real. He then becomes confused, because he neither knows the true character of the universe nor the cause of it.

Why creation? What is the purpose of it? The "how" has already been explained: the dominance of tamas guna occurring in the field of the Godhead and resulting in the manifestation of the universe. This is the creative process which occurs over and over again. Simplistic explanations of the purpose of creation have from time to time been given by philosophers, in order to pacify unenlightened intellects. "God was lonely, and so he created worlds and ensouled them in order to have companionship," is one such simplistic explanation. "God created the worlds and produced souls so that souls could have an opportunity to become conscious and reunite with God," is another theory sometimes expressed.

The Buddha, as well as other seers, declined even to respond to questions about how and why the worlds were framed. They declared such questions to be superficial and leading but to useless speculation. On the other hand, they asserted that it is possible to awaken from unconscious attachment to the relative spheres and to experience knowledge of the truth, liberation of consciousness. Pure consciousness is not in need of improving upon itself, and God, being self-complete, has no need to engage in the creation of world games in order to add to such completeness.

When the primal substance out of which all matter emerges was produced by the creative current, then, due to the influence of sattva guna, the brightening attribute, fine "heaven" realms were also produced. Subtle substance-matter continues to flow outward to manifest as the universe, and fine heaven realms become "resting places" for souls awakening from matter-bound consciousness to God-realization.

Heaven and hell are not places but states of consciousness which result in corresponding experiences. Heaven is the soul's experience when increasingly God-conscious. Hell is the soul's experience when, almost totally identified with matter, it feels itself hopelessly alienated from God. God does not reward us, and God does not punish us. Happiness and unhappiness are directly related to the soul's harmony with nature or its disharmony with nature. Suffering is due to conscious or unconscious failure to live in accord with natural laws. Life is impersonal and fairness exists, in that both the more conscious and the less conscious experience equally the results of their wise or unwise behavior. Those who are unwise can become wise—by entering into a purposeful process of transformation leading to spiritual awakening.

The Field of
Cosmic Mind (5)

The light of pure consciousness, shining upon the field of fine primal substance, enlivens it. This field of fine primal substance is called, in Sanskrit, *maya*, the fabric of which all nature is formed and by which nature is embellished. The blending of the light of pure consciousness and the field of primal substance results in the formation of a mind-stuff, often referred to as cosmic mind. What we refer to as our "minds" are particularized expressions of cosmic mind-stuff, but it is not exactly mind as we commonly understand it.

This mind-stuff is really a covering of consciousness. When consciousness relates to it and calmness results, it makes up *the sense of individualized consciousness.* When individualized consciousness becomes overly identified with matter, it assumes a *sense of separate existence*, or ego. Being identified with primal substance and sattva guna, and with tamas guna, this unit of consciousness becomes magnetized. One pole attracts it to the field of pure consciousness and the other attracts it to the field of creation. Thus, the *intellect* and the *mind* (thinking principle) are produced.

The mental sheath is the vehicle used by the soul during its involvement with the relative spheres. The ideal is for one to learn, through practice, to encourage calm mental states which will afford one the opportunity to experience the inner nature as distinct from the ego sense. During calm states one is also more likely to be able to exercise intelligence, the faculty of discernment. When the mental field is agitated, however, one is more likely to be confused, to be attracted to external matters, and to be anchored in the feeling of being separate from the source.

During quiet meditation, the light of pure consciousness is clearly discerned as reflected in the organ of intelligence. This is referred to as *buddhi*; it is from this term that the word *buddha*, or enlightened one, has evolved. Remember this axiom: There is nothing in the universe which is separate from the source, and there are no individual beings. The universe is Consciousness, manifesting *as* we behold it, and seeming individuals are reflections of the one light of pure consciousness.

A reflected ray of conscious light, unbound by attachments, is referred to as a son of God. With only enough identification with nature to experience a mild degree of "I-consciousness," such a soul is free to roam the fine spheres or heavens. When such a soul becomes overly identified with gross matter, however, tamas guna prevails and the soul loses its awareness of its divine nature to some degree and becomes deluded.

Our original involvement with matter occurred because rays of pure consciousness mixed with fine primal substance; we are here because of the impulse of life to express—we are here because of divine will. This is why some saints possessed of a devotional nature pray, "Lord, I did not ask to be involved in this world. It was your will that resulted in my involvement. Therefore, you are the one to awaken and redeem me. I surrender myself to your grace!" And, with complete surrender, souls become attracted to the source and experience spiritual awakening and inner realization.

Through the mind we use we have access to cosmic mind. We can think thoughts and see them manifested in the world because cosmic mind responds to our thoughts. It is possible to know everything that is contained in cosmic mind, and it is also possible to transcend cosmic mind entirely and to experience the absolute field, the field of pure consciousness. The ideal, when working creatively with cosmic mind, is to pray for inner guidance in order to know how best to think, how best to desire, and how best to express the divine will. Egocentric desires can lead to further confusion, while selfless desires can lead to the fulfillment of purposes and happiness.

Fifteen Mind-World
Connecting Principles (6—20)

Due to the influence of outflowing primal force, five aura electricities are produced from consciousness-awareness, the individualized essence. The five electricities (pranas) become the *root causes* of all else that is manifested. One aura electricity manifestation flows from the center and two each from the sides of the individualized essence, making five in number. These result in a magnetic field which is the faculty or organ of intelligence for the partially deluded soul.

The five electricities have attributes: sattva guna, manifesting in the organ of intelligence; tamas guna, predominating in mind (thinking principle); and rajas guna, which enables action to occur, allowing desires to be neutralized by satisfaction of them. From the attributes of the aura electricities are produced the fifteen mind-world connecting principles:

The *five organs of the senses* enable us to hear, touch, see, taste and smell. The *five organs of action* enable us to eliminate waste products, procreate, walk, speak, and exercise manual skills. The *five objects of the senses*: ether (hearing), air (touching), fire (seeing), water (tasting) and earth (smelling), when united with the organs of the senses, satisfy desires. These five objects of the senses are really subtle causes of material manifestation of the five elements. These fifteen connecting principles, together with intellect and mind, make

up the subtle body of the soul, the one which survives the
physical body at transition.

Five Elements of
Manifest Creation (21—25)

The five subtle-element influences (the objects of the
senses) when in combination produce the gross material world.
In the famous treatise by Shankara, Atma Bodh (Self-Knowl-
edge), we find, in verses 6—8:

> The world, filled with attachments and aversions,
> and the rest, is like a dream: it appears to be real as
> long as one is ignorant but becomes unreal when one
> is awake. The world appears to be real as long as non-
> dual Consciousness, which is the basis of it all, is not
> known. It is like any other illusion, having no basis of
> its own. All the various forms exist in the imagination
> of the perceiver, the substratum being the eternal and
> all-pervading Consciousness whose nature is existence
> and intelligence. Names and forms are like rings and
> bracelets and Consciousness is like the gold from which
> they are formed. As the all-pervading space appears to
> vary on account of its association with various forms
> (mental, electric, magnetic) which are different from
> each other, and remains pure upon the destruction of
> the form-giving qualities, so also the omnipresent Lord
> (Consciousness as creative manifesting power) appears
> to be diverse on account of His association with various
> form-building qualities and remains pure and one
> upon the dissolution of these qualities. Owing to its
> association with various restricting qualities and attri-
> butes, such ideas as differences, color and social posi-
> tion are superimposed on Supreme Consciousness, as
> flavor, color and worth are attributed to water. The
> physical body, the medium through which the soul
> experiences pleasure and pain, is determined by past
> actions and *formed out of the five great subtle ele-*
> *ments which become gross matter when one-half*

portion of one subtle element becomes united with one-eighth (portion) of each of the others. (Italics added.)

Governing principles in nature direct the formation of gross elements by combining subtle-element influences. According to Vedic sources, referred to by Shankara in his treatise, one-half of one subtle-element influence of ether, for instance, combines with one-eighth portion of air, fire, water and earth subtle-element influences to produce gross ether. One-half portion of subtle air-element influence combines with one-eighth portion of ether, fire, water and earth subtle-element influences to produce gross air, and so on, until gross ether, gross air, gross fire, gross water and gross earth elements are produced as material creation. Because of this each gross element also possesses minute portions of the other four elements. It is by understanding this process that some spiritual masters can transmute matter from one form to another and can "call forth" element influences from material substances to produce any type of matter.

In some commentaries on Samkhya philosophy only twenty-four categories of cosmic manifestation are enumerated, because they do not consider the unmanifest field to be a category. Other commentators include the unmanifest field as the beginning, as I have in this text, thus resulting in twenty-five categories. The outer twenty-four categories of creation constitute the entire realm of manifestation, from the Godhead through the material expression. Creation, then, is said to be a mere play of forces upon the background of the Godhead.

The Creation Story and the Seven Spheres

The seven spheres are realms, formed by the tensions and interactions of the polarities within the Godhead, influenced by the aura electricity attributes, or gunas. From the negative pole, force is repelled to produce the worlds; from the positive pole, an attracting influence redeems them. Primal substance covers, or veils, specialized units of Spirit, and the attracting influence unveils them. The seven spheres are the realms in which circumstances occur.

The Sphere of God — "This side" of the unmanifest field of pure consciousness is the Godhead; in the Godhead, because of polarities, are fine forces and attributes. Spirit, the field of pure consciousness, is devoid of attributes; the Godhead is a mixture of attributes. This sphere is known as *Satyaloka*, the sphere of truth or reality.

The Sphere of the Holy Spirit — This is the sphere where the impulse to manifest occurs. The Holy Spirit, the enlivening aspect of the Godhead, causes motion in the direction of creation and also regulates internal processes in creation.

The Sphere of Spiritual Reflection — The sphere where the sense of specialized existence occurs, when rays of pure consciousness shine on fine primal substance. This is where souls appear. They are not created, but are merely rays of pure consciousness partially influenced by identification with fine primal substance. This is the realm of the sons of God.

The Sphere of Initial Creation — The realm where fine primal substance mixes to manifest as: force, subatomic particles, space, and time. Here, too, is the realm of varied forces which emanate from the single force—electromagnetism, the force of gravity, the weak force, the strong force, and possibly other forces, such as anti-gravity.

The Sphere of Magnetism — Due to the influence of electric forces a magnetic field is produced. The specialized aspects of gross matter are not yet manifested.

The Sphere of Electric Attributes and Fine Matter — Here are to be found the subtle causes of the sense capacities, organs of action, and element influences which can result in material expression.

The Sphere of Gross Material Manifestation — This is the sense-perceived universe in which we presently dwell.

The creation story has been told in various ways over the centuries, and the accounts are similar. Let us examine The First Book of Moses, Called Genesis, the first book in the Bible (1:1—31):

In the beginning God created the heaven and the earth.

And the earth was without form, and void; and darkness was upon the face of the deep. And the spirit of God moved upon the face of the waters.

And God said, Let there be light: and there was light.

And God saw the light, that it was good: and God divided the light from the darkness.

And God called the light Day, the darkness he called Night. And the evening and the morning were the first day.

And God said, Let there be a firmament in the midst of the waters, and let it divide the waters from the waters.

And God made the firmament, and divided the waters which were under the firmament from the waters which were above the firmament: and it was so.

And God called the firmament Heaven. And the evening and the morning were the second day.

And God said, Let the waters under the heaven be gathered together unto one place, and let the dry land appear: and it was so.

And God called the dry land Earth; and the gathering together of the waters called he Seas: and God saw that it was good.

And God said, Let the earth bring forth grass, the herb yielding seed, and the fruit tree yielding fruit after his kind, whose seed is in itself, upon the earth: and it was so.

And the earth brought forth grass, and herb yielding seed after his kind, and the tree yielding fruit, whose seed was in itself, after his kind: and God saw that it was good.

And the evening and the morning were the third day.

And God said, Let there be lights in the firmament of the heaven to divide the day from the night; and let them be for signs, and for seasons, and for days, and years:

And let them be for lights in the firmament of the heaven to give light upon the earth: and it was so.

And God made two great lights; the greater light to rule the day, and the lesser light to rule the night: he made the stars also.

And God set them in the firmament of the heaven to give light upon the earth.

And to rule over the day and over the night, and to divide the light from the darkness: and God saw that it was good.

And the evening and the morning were the fourth day.

And God said, Let the waters bring forth abundantly the moving creature that hath life, and fowl that may fly above the earth in the open firmament of heaven.

And God created great whales, and every living creature that moveth, which the waters brought forth abundantly, after their kind, and every winged fowl after his kind: and God saw that it was good.

And God blessed them, saying, Be fruitful, and multiply, and fill the waters in the seas, and let fowl multiply in the earth.

And the evening and the morning were the fifth day.

And God said, Let the earth bring forth the living creature after his kind, cattle, and creeping thing, and beast of the earth after his kind: and it was so.

And God made the beast of the earth after his kind, and cattle after their kind, and every thing that creepeth upon the earth after his kind: and God saw that it was good.

And God said, Let us make man in our image, after our likeness: and let them have dominion over the fish of the sea, and over the fowl of the air, and over the cattle, and over all the earth, and over every creeping thing that creepeth upon the earth.

So God created man in his own image, in the image of God created he him; male and female created he them.

And God blessed them, and God said unto them, Be fruitful, and multiply, and replenish the earth, and subdue it; and have dominion over the fish of the sea, and over the fowl of the air, and over every living thing that moveth upon the earth.

And God said, Behold, I have given you every herb bearing seed, which is upon the face of all the earth, and every tree, in the which is the fruit of a tree yielding seed; to you it shall be for meat.

And to every beast of the earth, and to every fowl of the air, and to every thing that creepeth upon the earth, wherein there is life, I have given every green herb for meat: and it was so.

And God saw every thing that he had made, and, behold, it was very good. And the evening and the morning were the sixth day.

Matter-identified Spirit is veiled by five coverings or sheaths. These reflections of pure consciousness, when sheathed by various coverings, become involved with creation at different levels or spheres. Some remain on the other side of maya and function as radiant beings, as "gods and goddesses." Others become involved in grosser spheres and function according to prevailing circumstances. Many never become fully identified with earth realms except in rare instances when they do so for the purpose of accelerating the evolution of the planet upon which they function. This, too, is due to the will of God, as part of the grand process. When a fully illumined soul takes physical birth it is an *avatara* manifestation, an incarnation of God's power and light manifested in order to hasten man's redemption. Trillions of life units are sent into involvement with matter as part of the creation process, and these are responsible for the evidence of life which ensouls forms.

The five sheaths or coverings of the reflected lights of pure consciousness are as follows:

The Essence or Heart Sheath — That which enlivens is the heart, the essence of life. Because of its feeling nature it can experience tranquil awareness or bliss or *ananda*.

The Intelligence Sheath — Produced from aura-electricities, this is the seat of intellect, the ability to discern.

The Mind Sheath — Produced from the negative pole of the magnetic field formed by the aura-electricities, the mind sheath contains the subtle organs of the senses. Sensory input is presented to the intellect, which enables one to determine the evidence of what is perceived.

The Sheath of Prana or Life Force — This is commonly known as the astral body and contains the subtle roots of the organs of action (elimination, procreation, walking, talking and manual dexterity).

The Sheath of Gross Matter — The material universe, as well as the physical body of man. It is governed by inner principles which work from subtle and fine levels of creation. The physical body of man is nourished by food and, to some degree, by prana.

Creation unfolds from Consciousness. After full manifestation, as the attracting influence unveils various gross coverings, life appears when conditions are favorable. Life is present in latent form even in minerals and metals, and life is active in the subatomic particles which form the constituents of atoms.

As divine magnetism unveils life force, the organs of action begin to operate and plant life appears. As divine magnetism unveils the mind, the subtle organs of the senses become active; organisms, then more complex life forms, appear. In this way do life forms manifest on our planet, from early beginnings to man. The body of man is the most complex of all life forms, and through it the soul can awaken to God-realization. While intelligence expresses through all of nature, it is through man, because of his refined nervous system, that divinity can fully shine.

Through the use of certain procedures, a conscious person can quicken his spiritual evolution by being open to the ideal of awakening and by contributing to internal transformation. Man, then, is not blindly restricted by instinctual drives and karmic conditions. He can, through self-reflection and spiritual practices, contribute to beneficial changes in his mind, subtle bodies, and the physical body itself.

The intelligence of Consciousness has so arranged things that all living creatures are provided with the essentials for their survival and welfare. When harmony prevails, the balance of nature assures the opportunity for continued growth and unfoldment on Planet Earth.

TWO

The Soul's Journey
Through Space and Time

We have come into this world from inner space, and to inner space we will eventually return. Many people, not only those who are religious, have had moments when they felt themselves to be immortal, and when they felt immortal, that they were here in the body in order to have certain experiences, or for reasons which were not quite clear to them.

The essence of you, the essence of me, is immortal. This is so because we are units of pure consciousness identified with mind, body and matter, a circumstance which is not permanent. The truth of our being has been expressed many times, in different ways. The Bhagavad Gita expresses it this way (2:20—25):

> He who thinks the embodied One to be a slayer and he who thinks the embodied One to be slain, neither of them know correctly. The embodied One neither kills nor is He killed. He is never born nor does He die, nor having been, does He ever again cease to be. Unborn, eternal, perennial, this ancient One is not killed when the body is killed. He who knows this is imperishable, eternal, unborn, unalterable—how can that person kill and who can he kill or cause to be killed? As a man taking off worn out garments laters puts on new ones, similarly the Owner of the body, aban-

doning worn out bodies, enters into new ones. Weapons do not cleave Him, fire does not burn Him, the waters do not wet Him, nor does the wind dry Him. He is uncleavable, unburnable, cannot be made wet, nor can He be made dry; the eternal, all-permeating, absolute, and unmoving: He is the ancient One. He is unmanifest, is not the subject of thought, and is said to be incorruptible; therefore, knowing Him, it does not behoove you to grieve after anyone.

Souls come out from the inner planes and they retire to them for a duration of rest after a sojourn in the material realms. This cyclical process, known as reincarnation, can continue for thousands of years, until the soul removes itself from matter identification as the result of Self-realization or until the purpose for its involvement has been served.

The soul's journey through space and time is not a mystery to enlightened persons. It is only those who are grounded in materialism, those whose intellectual and intuitive faculties remain somewhat veiled, who consider it an unsolvable mystery. We have the testimony of scriptures and of conscious people to inform us on the matter. Therefore, the subject is not one to be debated, but is one to be examined by each of us until we arrive at our own clear understanding. It is only this understanding, as the result of Self-realization, which will satisfy the heart.

Souls become involved with the creation process for a variety of reasons. Most have come into involvement because of having been carried here, when the worlds were manifested, by the creative force responsible for projecting subtle matter into full expression. Becoming ensheathed in successive coverings (fine, intellectual, mental, astral and physical), the soul's innate power to know is somewhat suppressed. This is the initial delusion or unknowingness, and it results in incorrect or incomplete perception, errors in judgment, confusion, and the many problems which follow. The soul becomes mired in matter, and restrictions accumulate. These restrictions must either be removed or transcended by the soul desirous of conscious knowledge and liberation.

Simplistic explanations to the contrary, we are not placed here to be tested by God or to be given an opportunity to choose death or soul freedom. We are here because we are essential to the process of creation; when we are no longer essential to the evolutionary process we will awaken from the mortal dream and be restored to conscious perfection. God did not produce the worlds because "he was bored or lonely." The worlds unfolded from the Godhead because of the impulse to manifest, resulting in an outflow of creative force, the origin of the universe.

Until we awaken, we have purpose in this world and in whatever other, subtle spheres it will be our destiny to experience until final liberation. We are here to unfold, to learn, to serve the cause of world enlightenment and to engage in spiritual practices which can result in increasing knowledge and full God-realization. Many who have gone before us have shown us the way through precept and example, so we cannot say that we do not know what the solution to the riddle of life is, or how best to experience life ourselves.

The Web of Karma and How to Work Through It

The accumulation of restrictions, desires, conflicts, attitudes, beliefs, reaction habits, coping methods, and all else that is part of our conditioning, taken together represents our karmic condition. Unconscious man is, for the most part, almost totally at the mercy of his inner conditionings. He does not perceive clearly, he is driven by desires, he is egocentric, impelled by sense cravings, and at the mercy of drives, tendencies and impulses rooted in deeper levels of mind, emotional nature and body. *Karma* refers to action and reaction, to cause and effect in the universe and in man. Our inner conditionings result in thoughts, feelings and behavior which determine our general pattern of life experience. As we become increasingly conscious and discerning we are able to be more self-determined and less at the mercy of inner drives and conditionings.

When we experience strong desire, feel deep emotion, experience hurt, or accept a belief or opinion as true when it is not, impressions result in the mind and emotional body which influence future behavior. Too, because of the mind-body relationship, mental and emotional states cause changes in the physical structure, so that karmic traces become more deeply imbedded. Unusually painful or pleasurable experiences leave their mark; so much so that, later, even thinking about such experiences will cause them to be experienced in imagination again, with all of the intensity of the original events. Some especially traumatic experiences are often repressed, buried deep in the unconscious, and there they remain dormant until a future time, when they can be looked at and handled or else be restimulated and again be the cause of emotional upset and possible neurotic behavior.

A vast amount of suppressed material lies hidden in the chambers of the mind in many people, blocking creativity and darkening major portions of the mind. When heretofore hidden impressions stir and begin to surface we are often challenged to confront and come to terms with them. The more soul-aware we are, the easier it is for us to resolve threatening matters. It is from the vantage point of self-understanding that we are able to see karmic situations for what they are, merely recorded impressions of past events which really have no power of their own to unduly influence our states of consciousness, mental states or behavior.

Regular practice of superconscious meditation, a natural life style in harmony with the rhythms of the universe, and a sense of purpose in life will enable us to remove ourselves from the effects of potentially pain-causing karmic influences. It is important to remember that we need not be victimized by the results of past unwise or incorrect thinking or behavior. Too, as the result of spiritual awakening, when powerful flows of creative superconscious force flood mind and body, stored impressions in mind, emotional body and physical body will be "burned out," dissolved completely. The dissolving action may be mild, medium or intense. Sometimes a powerful spiritual awakening experience can result in the accumulated karmic impressions of many incarnations being erased entirely.

Other useful things to do besides regular meditation prac-

tice are: 1) seek out the company of persons who are living a
God-centered life; 2) cultivate the virtues (see chapter five);
3) engage in a life style which allows full opportunity for soul
actualization; and 4) perform all duties and all creative work
with the attitude that one is rendering service to God. In
these ways the effects of past errors are weakened and finally
neutralized.

Self-centered desire is a major factor in the accumulation
of karmic patterns. Strong desire, unless modified or neutralized, tends to fulfill itself. In this way many are self-bound to
the process of causation, to the revolving wheel of desire and
fulfillment of desire, which in turn leads to new desires.

What to do? We must desire in order to accomplish our
purposes, and there are basic urges which must be satisfied if
we are to live a natural life and fulfill our obligations. The key
is to do everything we do from a higher level of understanding,
to live a natural life but without compulsion and without being
a slave to cravings and sense urgings. One can be the master
of mental processes and regulate feelings and behavior; in this
way it is possible to live in the world but not be overly attached
to it. All actions performed in the right way and with the
correct attitude will enable us to fulfill our purposes without
binding us to unwanted future circumstances.

In the Bhagavad Gita (3:9) Krishna explains the basis of
bondage to his disciple, Arjuna:

> The world is the cause of bondage to karma, except
> for actions performed for the purpose of sacrifice.
> Therefore, perform actions for the sake of sacrifice
> and conduct yourself as free from attachment.

In this verse the word *sacrifice* refers to the ideal of performing all actions for the purpose of assisting the evolutionary
process, rather than in a self-serving way. This means that the
work one does should be constructive, useful to society, and
useful to the overall purpose for which creation exists. Understanding how to work, one can live a normal life, see to the
raising and education of children, enjoy social interaction,

pursue a variety of interests, and in all ways behave appropriately. In this way, even while involved with duties and relationships, one lives an harmonious and ever-increasingly God-aware life. Such a mode of life enables one to understand and work out personal karmic influences, while avoiding a heavy accumulation of further karmic impressions.

Not everything that happens to us is the result of long past causes. More often, what we experience in our world is due to our present state of consciousness and mental states. Much of what happens is dependent upon whether or not we are as conscious as we could be. If we are conscious and responsive we tend to relate intelligently and harmoniously to our environment. If we are unaware and reactive we tend to make mistakes and become victimized by unfolding circumstances. For instance, when we are conscious and responsive we can flow with whatever is presently unfolding, without injuring others or ourselves. When we are unaware, uncaring and reactive, we tend to be inattentive, inappropriate and destructive in thought, word and deed.

Birth and Death as Incidents
in the Soul's Journey to Discovery

Entry into this world, and departure from it, may be major events for the soul undergoing the experiences, but they are incidental occurrences when viewed from a more cosmic perspective. We are awed when birth occurs in nature and we are awed in the presence of death. The latter, because it serves as a reminder of our own physical mortality, is also often somewhat sobering. Perhaps at such moments we may dimly recall previous similar experiences we have had, or perhaps we are prompted to think of the years remaining to us in the present life cycle and what yet remains to be accomplished.

Concurrent with conception, when sperm and ovum unite, the soul's influence is present, its karmic condition influencing the nature of the developing form which will serve as its next physical body. The resulting infant form will then be a combination of: 1) genetic factors inherited from the parents; 2) the karmic influences (and soul awareness) of the newly incarnated soul; and 3) certain environmental influences present during the term of gestation. Even during womb existence the character of the mind and developing body are subject to the influence of the diet of the mother, conversations she has and which take place in her presence, events that occur about her, and the thoughts and attitudes of those to whom she relates. Is it no wonder, then, that each newborn child is unique, even to having a distinct personality!

Subtle-element governing principles also become influential at conception, to a large extent determining for the remainder of the newborn's life his or her basic physical and psychological constitution. There is also an astrological influence due to planetary radiations determined by their positions in the sky at the moment of conception and at the time of birth. To a discerning person, the horoscope can reveal indications of a person's karmic condition and general tendencies and trends in the life, but in this regard it should be remembered that karmic conditions are *not* fixed and that one should not assume a fatalistic stance when made aware of them. A person of superior realization is removed from most, if not all of the effects of both karmic and planetary influences. Sri Yukteswar, Paramahansaji's guru, would often examine the horoscope of a disciple and, after intuitive examination of the disciple's karmic condition, recommend a course of behavior to help in avoiding complications. He would sometimes advise the wearing of certain metals and gems for the purpose of balancing a person's energy field and to neutralize the effects of planetary radiations. Of this he said, "There are certain mechanical features in the law of Karma that can be skillfully adjusted by the fingers of wisdom."

Karmic influences can also be transmitted from one's parents and ancestors. There are two reasons for this: inherited tendencies, and tendencies communicated because of sympathetic mental and emotional rapport. Characteristics acquired by one's family predecessors leave their marks on the body, which are then passed on through the genetic material. In addition, if there is a close emotional family relationship, mental and emotional waves carry influences which can be received and acquired by children and grandchildren. This can reach for many generations.

It is likewise true that the superior realization of one family member can, because of mental-emotional rapport, beneficially influence ancestors as well as generations yet unborn. Such radiations of thought waves and spiritual influences are not limited to embodied souls in the family line, but can pass into the astral spheres as well. It is for this reason that some spiritual masters encourage their followers to pray for the welfare of their parents and of all in the family line who have preceded them. Even if one's prayer efforts do not affect those for whom one prays, the process itself is beneficial to the one who prays because it contributes to inner harmony and psychological health.

Ideally, a young person should be provided with a complete education to prepare for the adult period to follow. This should include all practical matters without sacrificing education in moral, ethical and spiritual matters. A youth should be reminded of his duties and obligations in this world and should be informed about the nature of Consciousness, the nature of the soul, and the nature and purpose of the world. In this way would a young person be fully prepared to live an ideal life in this world. Constructive latent tendencies would be awakened and a sense of destiny would be experienced.

We are all born with certain duties which are ours simply because we are here. These duties to self and others should be clearly understood and fulfilled with reverence and thankfulness. There are also duties which we assume by choice, and these should also be fulfilled correctly. Then, unless we have inherited wealth, we will have to learn how to adapt the resources available to us in the universe in order to see to our personal needs and accomplish our purposes. And, always, while growing into maturity we should remember that our basic responsibility is to increasingly be aware of the presence and reality of God.

For most people in society, after the educational phase and the years of work and child raising, the next phase should be devoted to public service, according to one's means and

capacities. The later years may be given more to deeper meditation and contemplation, in preparation for departure from
this world.

As the moment of transition approaches, ideally there will
be an inner knowing about the impending event and a natural
inclination to make final practical arrangements and to withdraw from external involvement. Transition will then occur
naturally, without trauma or confusion. Just as we came into
the world, we will one day leave it. When we depart, depending
upon our state of consciousness, we will move into an astral
sphere, a causal sphere, the sphere of God, or we will dissolve
the sense of individual identity entirely and rest in the ocean
of pure consciousness.

It may be, as we begin the transition phase, that we become
increasingly aware of the presence of God, and of the benevolent presence of supportive friends who come to assist us.
Many people have testified to having seen and communicated
with "shining beings" while hovering near the borderline between this and the inner planes. Some who have temporarily
slipped from the body, after an accident or during a major illness, have reported how peaceful it is in the light realm they
experienced, and that radiant beings were there to nurture
and advise them. Sometimes relatives who have undergone
transition long before are there to welcome the soul newly
awakening to astral or celestial experience. One who is devotional, and who has been a spiritual aspirant, may be welcomed
by members of his or her spiritual family. Paramahansaji often
said that disciples of his tradition would, at the time of their
transition, be met by a representative of the guru line who
would "usher them into the infinite."

I know that while Paramahansaji was embodied he would
often, while in meditation, work with disciples who were
making their transition and help them in the process. He was
also effortlessly in communication with many disciples and
with various saints who roamed the inner spheres.

Paramahansaji counseled us not to attempt communication
with those in subtle realms if our motives were rooted in selfishness or emotional need. He stressed the ideal of "working out

our salvation" by attending to duties and by deepening our spiritual practices. "Masters," he said, "do not work through mediums. After I am gone from this world do not go to a medium and expect to contact me that way. I will never communicate through a medium. Nor do any of the masters."

For centuries past, and it is also common today, persons have claimed to be "channels" through whom enlightened beings speak from other planes. Such persons are either deluded, if they are sincere, or else fraudulent. In either instance it is best for a spiritual aspirant to have nothing to do with their activities. Those who persist in looking for a "medium" through whom wisdom can be channeled are usually emotionally immature and lacking in sufficient self-responsibility to embark upon a useful program of discipline, study and meditation, a program which could be the means of their spiritual awakening and ultimate enlightenment.

The astral sphere is comprised of a universe which is much larger than our physical universe. It contains astral suns and heavenly bodies, and many planets to which souls go to continue their unfoldment. Some astral planes are inhabited by souls which are radiantly conscious and which experience paradise-like circumstances. Because of the difference in vibrational frequency, souls in the lower astral realms cannot have access to the more rarified realms. They may spiritually awaken and then move to the higher astral realms or they may reincarnate to continue their spiritual evolution.

Since spiritual unfoldment can continue in the astral realms, it is not always necessary for souls to return to Earth, unless their destiny or their karmic needs demand they do so. Millions of souls move from this sphere to the astral sphere, and back again, driven by need, desire or curiosity. Billions more continue their upward way, from lower astral to higher astral experiences, then on to causal and celestial spheres.

If a soul is to be reborn in this world it may do so a few months after leaving it for the astral sphere, or it may spend a long duration in astral experience before returning. There is no fixed rule about this, as it is determined by the soul's state of consciousness and its destiny. Time is not perceived in the same way in the astral sphere as it is in our universe; seeming thousands of years of experience might pass in the astral sphere while only a few solar years might pass in our world.

In the lower astral realms life is experienced much as it is here, and many do not experience much difference, because they are not that much different in their understanding. In the more rarified astral realms there is greater freedom of expression because inner restrictions have been transcended. Astral beings there can travel from one astral planet to another with speeds faster than electric current or radio waves. They can dematerialize and rematerialize their astral bodies, appear to be older or more youthful, and manipulate their environment through intention. Knowing that their realm is composed of prana, they can change the environment at will, through visualization and will power. Many become so enthralled by their surroundings, and their abilities, that they neglect their spiritual aspirations and roam almost endlessly through the corridors of astral space. Souls can "die" to the astral realm and either be born into a new physical body on this plane or experience transition to the finer causal sphere. Some causal planes are accessible only to souls which are nearly God-conscious. Here they spend their time in communion and absorption in pure consciousness. After a duration they shed their causal sheath and merge in God.

In the astral and causal spheres are illumined masters who work with souls seeking permanent freedom from all restriction. Such illumined masters are able, when necessary, to transport themselves to higher astral realms and even to the Earth realm to assist souls in need. Having inwardly realized the dream-like character of creation they are not restricted by any aspect of it; for them no barriers exist.

Souls, being rays of pure consciousness, are neither male nor female. The qualities of maleness and femaleness manifest when souls become involved with fine primal substance and begin their descent into matter. While possessing characteristics common to their acquired sexual role, all embodied souls are essentially the same in their true nature and have the same potential for creative expression and Self-realization.

It is not true that souls incarnate alternately as male and female in order to acquire experience and learn lessons. Phenomenal realm experience is not essential to Self-realization. Enlightenment is a matter of awakening, not of learning through experience.

For many, the most challenging task is to learn to wisely use the senses while relating to the astral and physical realms. This is because of the tendency for attention to flow out and become overly involved with externals. There is nothing wrong or "sinful" in sense experience. It is through the senses that we relate to our environment and to others. The problem comes when there is excessive involvement in sensuous relationships which can, in turn, result in emotional confusion and attachment to the objects of desire.

The solution is self-discipline, the observance of spiritual disciplines and deep meditation. When balance is achieved between the inner and outer realms, one naturally flows through the world appropriately and without unwise attachment.

Meditators "die daily" in God. By reversing the flow of attention and life force in the body from the senses to the spiritual eye, the meditator feels life currents ascend the spinal pathway, through the chakras, to merge in the light and in the sound of Aum. It is in this way that one prepares for eventual transition from the body, so that when the moment comes for him to do it, he does so without regret and without any unfinished business in the world.

By consciously controlling attention and life force during the years prior to transition the process of departure is made easy. As the result of living a conscious disciplined life, without attachments and in surrendered faith, much physical, astral and causal karma is removed and transcendence is then possible. Even if, upon leaving the body, all karma has not been eradicated, the soul will soar to greater heights as a result of having prepared ahead of time. Then, should one return to this world he will be spiritually advanced when he arrives and able to continue his awakening experience with no major resistance to be met and overcome.

Until final liberation, it is important that we be focused

on the goal. Even advanced souls, if they waver, can stray from the path and even fall back into bad habits for a duration.

It is the ultimate destiny of every soul to awaken in God. God, the Cosmic Dreamer, is playing all roles in, and as, creation. It is by learning to see through appearances and identifying with the Dreamer of dreams that we are released from suffering due to ignorance. By faithfully living in harmony with the laws of nature (living a righteous life) we are saved from fear of the things of this world, and from fear of death and after-death states.

Do We Meet the Same People Over and Over Again, in this and Other Realms?

Because of either a karmic relationship or a shared destiny, we often move through space and time with kindred souls. It is not uncommon for family members to continue in the astral realms their relationships started in this world. This is not necessary, but it often happens because of affection and/or karmic ties. If relationships continue because of karmic ties they will often be severed when mutual karma is dissolved. Sometimes relationships based on need can blossom into spiritual friendships and a sharing of mutual soul destiny.

Sometimes persons in conflict with one another will continue to compete until their mutual differences are dissolved, or they may continue to meet others with similar tendencies and, in this way, be given the opportunity to do whatever must be done to overcome such challenges.

On the spiritual path, especially, bands of souls share a common destiny. This is obviously true in the instance of the guru-disciple relationship, because it is the guru's responsibility to assist disciples until they are liberated. Too, if the guru has a world mission, his disciples will incarnate during his earth sojourn and assist him with his mission, while continuing their own spiritual practices.

I was once walking with my guru during the early evening at his desert retreat near Twenty-Nine Palms, California. I asked, "Sir, have I been with you before?" I knew the answer, but sought his reassurance.

Paramahansaji said, "How could you be with me now if you had not been with me before? You came to help me with this work. You have been with me many times in the past and you will be with me many times in the future." After a pause, he continued: "You almost made it last time. You only have one or two little things to take care of this time."

Shortly before Paramahansaji left the body (on March 7, 1952), he informed us that his time on Earth was up. He had finished the work he had come to do this time. Two months and two days before his *mahasamadhi*, his conscious transition, at a gathering of disciples who had come together for his birthday celebration, he said that when he left us he would rest for a while and then return to be with Babaji in the Himalayas. He said that he would watch over his disciples, and observe the unfoldment of his work. He further said that he would see many of us again but that we might not recognize him. He gave us a hint when he said, "My colors will be blue and gold." Blue and gold were two of his favorite colors when he was with us, and he frequently used them when decorating buildings and chapels.

A reading of various world scriptures, and biographical accounts of more contemporary saints, reveals that gurus almost always attract disciples to them who have been with them before. From among the many who were attracted to Jesus, for example, he called forth a few whom he recognized, and "opened he their understanding."

Our emphasis, while here, should not be to leave the world; it should be to "overcome" the world by experiencing a conscious relationship with it. So long as there is purpose for our being involved with creation, the Creator will see to it that we are. Even so, with understanding and Self-realization, wherever we are we will be consciously anchored in God and all will be well.

THREE

Responsibilities of Discipleship

The path of discipleship is easily understood and accepted by those spiritual aspirants who are ready for the responsibility of focusing attention and energies in the direction of Self-realization. It is not understood or welcomed by persons who are emotionally immature and therefore unwilling to enter into the program of discipline which is necessary if transformation is to be experienced.

True disciples are able to surrender to God's will and to do their utmost to enter into a conscious relationship with life. Those who are not ready for discipleship either do not even consider the possibility, or else engage in superficial analysis and attempt to dismiss the usefulness of discipleship. Yet the tradition of discipleship has persisted through the ages because it has been found to be essential. Unawakened man is in need of guidance and encouragement. More, he is in need of soul quickening, so that the Holy Spirit can become influential.

I will here explain the path of discipleship so that any reasonably intelligent person can understand it. Those who are not yet ready to commit themselves to the disciplined life will, after reading this, have the opportunity to know what to expect when called to commitment.

Jesus stated the matter clearly (St. John 8:31, 32): "If ye continue in my word, then are ye my disciples indeed;

And ye shall know the truth, and the truth shall make you free." To "continue in the word" is to live in accord with the guidelines taught by enlightenment masters. A further, esoteric, meaning is to remain absorbed in the creative sound current (the Aum) during deep meditation.

God, the higher power, the cosmic Self of each of us, is the true guru, the light that removes darkness from mind and consciousness. God directs us through the workings of the Holy Spirit, His life which pervades the cosmos. God also guides us through the example and wise words of the embodied guru, if we have entered into such a relationship. The guru-disciple relationship is not one in which domination or exploitation occurs. One's guru, being perfected in Yoga, has no personal desire to play the role of guru; he or she merely does it as duty, to assist seekers on the path and to assist the process of world transformation.

Paramahansaji used to say, "If you will allow me, I will reveal God to you." That is the way with gurus—they can and do extend the invitation to Self-realization but they cannot unduly persuade. It is up to the devotee to respond to the call of God, to repent, to be committed, and to follow through with recommended processes.

Novice aspirants are often fearful of making a commitment on the path. They may be afraid because they fear their inability to abide by guidelines and recommendations. They may fear change, for change there must be on the awakening path. However, by the cultivation of devotion to God, one's natural instinct to know God is unfolded so that surrender comes more easily.

The guru's responsibility, once he has accepted a disciple, is to continue to work with that disciple until final results are experienced. The disciple may stray; he may be unfaithful to his commitment, or unable to fulfill his own aspirations, but the guru will not waver in his love and caring for the disciple. The guru-disciple bond, if it is real, is sealed in heaven and cannot be broken once it is established.

The disciple's responsibility is to listen to the guru's advice, accept initiation into meditation practices, and live an ideal life to the best of his ability. We are never asked to do the impossible, only to do our best. It is in this way that we rise higher and higher and eventually pierce the veil which for so long has obscured our perception of reality.

In the guru-disciple relationship mutual respect must prevail. Because the guru sees more clearly than the disciple, his words relating to spiritual unfoldment must be considered to be infallible. The guru, having undergone the experiences of discipleship himself, and having become fit to play the guru role by virtue of his enlightenment, knows the spiritual path thoroughly. He can point out the quickest ways to transformation and often see the disciple's needs more clearly than can the disciple himself. The disciple's spiritual evolution is considerably quickened because of his attunement with God through the guru.

The guru not only guides the disciple, according to the latter's temperament, capacity and need, he also infuses the disciple with his own consciousness and life force. This infusion of consciousness and life force creates a powerful soul bond between them and awakens spiritual forces in the disciple. The guru also intercedes, in thought, word and deed (usually during meditation) on behalf of the disciple. At times, through superior realization, the guru can remove inner karmic restrictions from the disciple's subtle body and mental field. At times he can elevate the disciple's consciousness so that a degree of God-consciousness is experienced. I have, at times, experienced this when in the company of Paramahansaji, and while being inwardly attuned to my guru line during meditation.

When attunement exists between guru and disciple, even if they are separated in space or by spheres, the divine magnetism flowing through the guru causes deep internal changes resulting in the awakening of kundalini in the disciple. Then the disciple is taught how to respond to this dynamic activity and to allow it to purify all of the coverings of the soul as well as the mental field.

It must be remembered that the major function of the guru is to encourage the disciple's increasing realization of God.

There may be advice, too, regarding the disciple's personal responsibilities and his duties to others and to society in general. The total process is one which will enable the disciple to fulfill his personal destiny and experience final liberation of consciousness.

The process may not always be an easy one. There may be occasions when the disciple is severely challenged when forced to confront his motives, his priorities, his behavior and his deepseated psychological conditionings. But this is what the discipleship path is all about; it is about transformation leading to enlightenment.

Jesus had strong words for those who were called to discipleship with him. In one instance (St. Luke 14:26) we read: "If any man come to me, and hate not his father, and mother, and wife, and children, and brethren, and sisters, yea, and his own life also, he cannot be my disciple." He was not using the word "hate" to mean rejection; it was meant to emphasize that God must be first in one's life, and then all other relationships will be appropriate.

In the same chapter (verse 27) we read: "And whosoever does not bear his cross, and come after me, cannot be my disciple." To paraphrase: "That person who does not attend to all of his disciplines and who is not willing to go through the fires of transformation, cannot be a true disciple."

Finally, in verse 33, we read: "So likewise, whosoever he be of you that forsaketh not all that he has, he cannot be my disciple." The teaching is clear: we cannot be successful on the spiritual path if we are double-minded, if we are confused and have mixed loyalties. It is not by literally departing from our relationships and possessions that we are able to realize our God nature; it is when we renounce outer attachments in order to know God that we are able to live in harmony with our God-created world.

Once our destined path is clear to us we should not waver from it. Others may follow another path, one which is in accord with their destiny, the one that is most useful for them. While the essential teachings of all enlightenment teachers are the same, the procedures may vary, and the frequency of energy shared by a guru line will be unique to that line. This is why we should be true to the path we feel to be our own. If we stray, if we attempt to incorporate practices not common to our destined line of gurus, we will adulterate our energies, rendering them impure so that our attunement with the guru line is impaired. It is not that our chosen way is right and that other ways are of less value; it is rather that purity is essential if we are to receive the subtle waves of grace which flow through the guru and those who preceded him.

It may be that a guru represents no guru line, but this is rare. It is more common that the guru line can be traced back thousands of years and that the teaching today is just as pure as it has been for centuries. This is because of careful instruction on the part of gurus in succession and because of the flow of divine force which is transmitted through the guru line, the force which has origins in the Godhead.

In today's awakening world many seekers will be drawn into a guru-disciple relationship for the first time and, in this way, become members of a growing spiritual family. Many disciples will be drawn into a relationship which began in the past, and theirs is a continuing process with the enlightenment tradition of destiny.

An important involvement with the guru is to assist him with his mission. His mission is to awaken souls and show them the way to Self-realization. No disciple ever has to ask, "My guru has his mission—now what is mine?" The disciple's obligation is to assist the guru with his mission; in this way, he discovers his own role in the cosmic process.

It is possible, even with the support of the guru, for a person to fall back into old ways and habits and temporarily stray off the spiritual path. If this occurs, it is due to the disciple's own ego-driven willfulness, the major "sin" or error which contributes to pain and suffering. There is no need for a disciple to make such a mistake. All that is required of him is faith in scripture, faith in the words of the guru, faith in the transformation process, and faith in the goodness of God.

A disciple should study and understand the principles which underlie the creation process. He should study and understand the true nature of God, the soul, and the way to Self-realization. Then, armed with knowledge and devoted to practice, he is certain to be successful on the path. With unfoldment, beliefs will give way to knowledge, confusion to certainty, and aimlessness to purposeful creative involvement with the evolutionary process.

Knowledge is grounded in Consciousness. It is subjective. It is within and may seem to come from above, as described in the Bhagavad Gita by Sri Krishna (15:1—5):

> Sages speak of the imperishable mystic tree, with roots above and branches below. The fruitage of this insight is clear perception which enables a person to know the truth in scriptures. The branches of this mystic tree extend below and above, nourished by the tendencies in nature, while the object of the senses is the twigs, and karma results, which binds man to action in the physical worlds. A wise person can cut off this tree (with its attachments to the world) with the strong sword of non-attachment. The way to freedom is to seek awareness of the True Source of all things, from which has come forth this cosmic process known as the universe. Seekers of truth who are free from pride, delusion and unreasoned attachment to things, who are ever devoted to the will of God and who have risen above the relativities and dualities, experience liberation of consciousness.

FOUR

Illumination and Liberation
of Consciousness

All of us, from time to time, become aware of the fact that the sense-perceived world is not really as it seems. We often intuitively sense the illusory character of creation, even when we cannot clearly comprehend what it is we are feeling. The reason for this is twofold: one, we possess at the soul level an innate knowledge of the life process; two, we become aware of the fact that we are never able to truly know our world through the senses because what is revealed to the senses is scanty and must be interpreted and then decided upon by the intellect, based upon incomplete or inaccurate sensory information. Such musings about the nature of reality can, however, be the beginning of a quest that will ultimately result in our being led to a path of study and spiritual practice which will enable us to finally realize the total truth about life.

For this, the average seeker needs to have his devotional nature aroused and also to have access to clear, accurate information about the nature of Consciousness. He may also require instruction in how-to-live principles and in the art of prayer and meditation. Fortunate is the novice who quickly connects with the right teacher or teaching tradition, the one which can enable him to begin his studies with a minimum of wasted effort! Not every teacher who is available to the public is competent to teach, no matter what his or her followers claim about the matter, and not every new seeker is prepared to receive clear instruction, even when such is available.

How does one find the right teacher, the right tradition, the one which is best for one's purposes? The answer is basic: one must first prepare oneself—by examining motives, by adopting a constructive life style, by minimizing ego drive, and by much sincere prayer and meditation. In this way one will surely be led to the right contact and be able to recognize it as such when it occurs.

If, through the force of constructive karma and God's grace, one should be led immediately to a true guru, one who is established in inner realization, this would be the most fortunate event possible. As a result of this contact the seeker would be shown, by precept and example, how to direct his attention inward through the process of meditation, and how to flow it back to the source of life within the body, the spiritual eye. This point is the connecting door between the outer and inner realms. This process of inward turning is within reach of every devotee who is sincere on the enlightenment path.

Moving attention and life force from without to within, then through the spiritual eye, is the esoteric way to soul freedom. Upon moving through the spiritual eye one's consciousness expands, because it is no longer identified with the physical body. Functioning through the astral body, enlivened by flows of prana, the devotee may have access to astral perceptions. Moving through the astral sphere one may have causal perceptions. Moving through the causal sphere, the soul becomes aware of celestial realms. Beyond them is the realm of God and the field of pure consciousness.

By dissolving awareness in Aum, the primal sound current, the meditator begins his journey Godward. While under the influence of tamas guna, the soul's attention is carried outward into contact with gross matter. When under the influence of the attracting magnetic current which pulls his attention Godward, the devotee experiences grace, which lifts him above all material ties. This is the true repentance, the flowing back to the source. This is the true spiritual baptism of which Jesus spoke (St. John 3: 5,6): "Verily, verily, I say unto thee, Except a man be born of water and of the Spirit, he cannot enter into the kingdom of God. That which is born of the flesh is flesh, and that which is born of the Spirit is spirit."

Being born of *water* means to be born into a physical form composed of the elements of nature, that is: ether, air, fire, water and earth. Being born of the Spirit results in soul quickening and subsequent awakening. Identified with the flesh, with material substance, we think ourselves to be material beings. Being awakened to the reality of Spirit we become aware of the fact of our true nature, that we are rays of pure consciousness. As rays of pure consciousness we can consciously experience God.

After spiritual awakening one has but to regulate one's life according to the guidelines given by the masters and surrender to God's grace. When this is done, everything else then occurs spontaneously. It is impossible for a person who is in harmony with the way of righteousness, and who is surrendered, to fail on the spiritual path. Unfoldments may not be humanly predictable but they will be in divine order. In time, one will "see through" the fabric of nature; one will see it for what it is, a play of lights and shadows occurring in the field of God *as* creation. Illumination, enlightenment, total comprehension as the result of direct experience, then follows.

Liberation of consciousness is experienced when one realizes the soul nature to be none other than pure consciousness. Before this, one may feel himself to be a reflection of the light of pure consciousness, as the light shines in the intelligence principle of the subtle sheath. With liberation, however, the soul knows itself to *be* that ray of pure consciousness, and it is aware of the boundless field of pure consciousness, from which all rays of light emanate. It is then that the soul is redeemed from material identification forever.

Prior to this realization, one may have momentary glimpses of reality, and momentary experiences of pure consciousness. One may even be able to live from the realization of pure being, while embodied, and still have to contend with karmic impressions remaining in the mental, astral and causal sheaths.

These remaining traces of karma can be exhausted or dissolved through experience and Self-realization, or they can be shed when the body is shed at transition. This awareness of inner reality while yet functioning through mind and body is the spiritual condition of many saints. They are therefore inwardly serene even while continuing to experience in the sphere in which they reside. Established in God-consciousness, their karmic traces are not binding, but merely represent occasional challenges and opportunities for understanding and transcendence.

At this stage one may be referred to as a liberated soul even while embodied, because inner illumination is constant and the existence of karmic traces does not represent a threat to such realization. An understanding of this condition can help us understand why some saints, who are unquestionably anchored in God-realization, still exhibit personality traits and occasionally face inner and outer challenge because of the working out of subtle karmic patterns. Some saints have experienced martyrdom, deprivation, illness and misunderstanding because of certain karmic conditions prevailing, even though their inner realizations were not diminished. This is not to assert that every person on the enlightenment path must emulate the difficulties of some saints; it is rather a matter of individual fate and destiny.

In order to accelerate changes in world consciousness, some saints have purposely overworked the body and pushed against public opinion, even while knowing that this would result in difficulties for themselves. This is done only under inner guidance, not out of any compulsion, and the inner awareness is in no way influenced by outer circumstances.

Being under the influence of the Holy Spirit, the awakening soul becomes Christed, anointed of God. Thereafter the soul moves through all the spheres, if this is the direction of the Holy Spirit, as a fully illumined being, knowing that it is in God and God is in it. The inner realization is established in God and the soul is no longer subject to the influence of maya, primal substance, the fabric of nature.

The Awakening Soul's
Natural Inclination

By becoming aware, even in part, of the insubstantial character of creation, and knowing that bondage is the result of lack of knowledge, an aspirant on the spiritual path desires release from bondage and seeks a way to enlightenment. Persisting in the right way, the soul eventually experiences salvation, freedom from bondage. The basic problem, common to all unenlightened people, is delusion due to lack of understanding. As mentioned earlier, because of errors in perception the deluded soul assumes the phenomenal realms to be permanent and the reality behind them to be nonexistent. The only solution to the problem is spiritual awakening and Self-realization. Philosophical speculation may entertain the mind but it will never satisfy the heart, the essence of the embodied soul. Sages are fond of counseling, "Seek out the truth in the heart." What they are saying is, "Seek out your real essence, that which is behind mind, feeling nature and body. Seek out that which enlivens mind, feelings and body. That which is the essence of you is eternal, nonchanging being."

The real essence can be discerned through right use of the purified intellect and it can be experienced by assuming the right viewpoint, by coming back to the center instead of being involved in outer matters entirely.

Let us examine the process of soul confusion more carefully:

Initial Unknowingness — As we have seen in chapter one of this section, primal substance, or maya, is endowed because of polarity with two major influences: The outflowing influence produces grosser expressions of itself and veils life units, causing them to be somewhat unconscious. This results in ego (the sense of individuality) and persistence to remain involved. The polarity influence results in attachments (attraction) and aversion (repulsion).

Persistence in involvement with the objective realms is due to the false belief that they alone exist. Attachment causes us to seek out objects of supposed happiness and aversion causes us to avoid circumstances which we think will contribute to unhappiness. In this way the unaware soul remains involved with matter.

The Way to Knowledge — By seeking to understand what is behind the appearances of the manifest realms we learn to discriminate between the inner and the outer, between causes and effects, and in this way we experience unfoldment on the spiritual path.

The polarity aspects of primal substance give rise to two characteristics: form-producing and truth-veiling. Forms of nature are manifested out of the field of primal substance; nothing in form exists which is not made out of primal substance. Truth, knowledge of Consciousness, is innate to Consciousness, but when units of pure consciousness are identified with matter they flow outward instead of remaining self-aware, and thus they consciously "forget" their true origin and nature for a duration. Because of the influence of delusion, egoism, attachment, aversion and continued identification with matter, the soul continues to roam in space and time in a confused state; no permanent happiness can then be experienced.

The desire to experience pure existence, pure consciousness, and changeless contentment is innate to every person. This is because these experiences are natural to the unfettered soul and the inner awareness of being, consciousness and contentment resides beneath the confusions of the mind. When we are settled in being, internal complications subside and soul virtues naturally unfold. When we are settled in conscious realization of our real nature we experience permanent fulfillment, not because of the absence of challenge but because we are restored to understanding.

The cultivation of evenmindedness is the first step in the direction of permanent contentment. For this, one needs a dispassionate nature, free from strong likes and dislikes. This is not the same as aversion, being repelled by the world; it is a matter of seeing all things in correct perspective, without being overly emotionally moved by circumstances. It was this that was taught by the Buddha to his disciples as being basic to the spiritual path. Evenmindedness is emphasized by all enlightenment teachers, because without the correct view of the world, and without appropriate relationships, one is almost certain to either become obsessed with things and circumstances or to tend to withdraw entirely. Accepting what occurs without being emotionally upset and being engaged in purposeful work without compulsion or attachment contributes to contentment. From the foundation of a contented life one is then able to pursue studies and meditation practice with an undistracted mind. This can lead to insight and direct experience of higher reality. In the Yoga Sutras (2:26) we read:

> The means of removing lack of knowledge is to remain firmly in the conscious knowledge of the truth regarding the relationship between pure consciousness and nature.

It is not possible to remain firmly in the consciousness of such knowledge when the passions are governing mind and senses. Therefore, the cultivation of contentment is recommended.

Our resolve to remain inwardly content is nourished by our studies, for by faithfully reading the words of wise people we are instructed and motivated to a higher life. Deep meditation on a regular schedule also enables us to become steady in contentment because of the inner stability experienced during superconscious perception. With increasing inner realization, and with the balancing of internal forces, we are naturally inclined to remain calm and insightful all of the time. As a result of surrender to God moral courage is awakened, enabling us to more easily persist along the course of right action. Vedic seers have an axiom:

> Some consider the deities to exist in the natural elements while the learned consider them to exist in the astral heavens; the unwise seek them in images and symbols, but the Yogi realizes God in the sanctuary of his own Self.

FIVE

The Way to Supreme
Realization

The soul's desire is to consciously rest in the awareness of itself. The Self is pure and self-complete because it is a perfect expression of God. Until this realization is experienced, no person can know full satisfaction. If full satisfaction could be known through any other means, many people would be satisfied today, but there cannot be truly contented people in the worlds if inward experience of God is lacking.

Through the cultivation of devotion and the awakening of our inborn capacities, we become inspired to extend our awareness and to do whatever is necessary to awaken from the mortal dream. Through devotion alone it is possible to know the reality of God but very few, even among sincere devotees, have single-pointed devotion. Therefore, as the result of revelation and practice, techniques and procedures have evolved which are helpful to the seeker on the enlightenment path. By doing certain things in the proper way, restricting influences can be weakened and dissolved and soul awareness can be released to explore the full range of Consciousness.

By modeling one's life after the pattern of the saints one can learn through experience how to live in accord with the laws of nature and how to open oneself to divine influences. No matter what our present condition in life may be, no matter what has happened to us in the past, no matter what our present level of understanding, if we will do certain things we will surely progress in the direction of higher knowledge.

Let us remember that nothing we do can *cause* enlightenment, because enlightenment is our natural condition when
obstructions are removed. If enlightenment were the effect of
any cause, it would fade when the momentum of cause influence ceased. Therefore, whatever we do in the way of spiritual
practice is for the purpose of *allowing* the inner nature to
unfold and express. As we persevere in our dedicated practices
all of the soul capacities emerge naturally, spontaneously,
and in divine order.

Basic and important to every person on the enlightenment
path is the living of a natural life, the cultivation of the
virtues, and an inward yearning to know the truth about life.
If we attend to these things, and meditate deeply, satisfactory
results must follow. In the Bhagavad Gita (16:1—3) we are
given an idea of the virtues to be cultivated:

> Courage, purity of mind, wise use of knowledge, con-
> centration, self-control and right use of abilities, along
> with faithful study of scriptures and noble purpose,
> non-violence, truth, freedom from anger, renuncia-
> tion, tranquillity, freedom from finding fault, com-
> passion to all, freedom from envy, gentleness, quiet
> manner and faithfulness, vigor, forgiveness, persist-
> ence, selflessness, freedom from the desire to do harm
> to another, and freedom from excessive pride—these
> are the natural endowments of a person who is born
> with a divine nature.

It is a rare person who is born with all of these qualities
fully actualized. By giving careful attention to our thoughts,
feelings and behavior, however, we can in time unfold these
qualities in ourselves, because they are natural to the soul.

By cultivating the virtues and living a moral life, all of the
inner restrictions which inhibit soul expression are dissolved.
A few of the more obvious effects of egoism are: hatred,
shame, fear, grief, condemnation, race prejudice, family pride,
and a smug sense of self-righteousness. The removal of these

alone would result in a person becoming psychologically healthy and an ideal representative of desirable qualities in society. The removal of destructive qualities and the actualization of divine qualities opens the door to salvation.

Because of the absence of internal disturbing influences it becomes easier for one to practice spiritual disciplines. One is able to sit in a relaxed posture, practice *pranayama*, turn the attention and life force inward and experience serene meditation. Through the correct use of pranayama, internal systems are balanced and all forces are directed to the spiritual eye, resulting in the opening of that inner gateway to divine revelation. By completely internalizing nerve currents total mental satisfaction is experienced so that one is no longer inclined to seek satisfaction in outer circumstances. One can then enjoy life without being driven by sense needs and without feeling separated from God.

By the correct use of pranayama the involuntary nerves are refreshed, decay processes in the body are suspended, and the advanced meditator acquires control over death. Many spiritual masters have demonstrated their ability to leave the body at will, during temporary excursions in subtle realms and at the moment of final transition. Some have also literally resurrected the physical form, for special purposes, and have appeared in a subtle body to instruct and encourage disciples. This is not a severe challenge to one who fully understands that the body is comprised of electric forces, prana and subtle-element influences held together by desire or will.

Jesus the Christ raised his body after it had been placed in a tomb, and later appeared to his disciples in a resurrected and transformed body. He appeared the same to some disciples, different to others, and at times was seen to move through closed doors. Sri Yukteswar, three months after his transition on March 9, 1936, appeared to Paramahansaji in a hotel room in Bombay, India. During that lengthy visitation Sri Yukteswar explained many things to his disciple, describing the astral and causal realms and sharing several prophecies about planet Earth, many of which have already unfolded.

During surrendered meditation, when internal forces are

flowing to the source, a true understanding of the nature of
God arises in the mind. This is followed by *samadhi*, the
calming of the mental waves, and direct experience of God
follows. This is the simple, natural scientific process of becoming aware of the divine nature. Even an agnostic, if he
will practice according to directions, will become God-realized.
Even if devotion is lacking in the beginning, if one will practice correctly, merely to experiment, results will be more
than satisfactory.

After a duration of dedicated practice, the magnetic attracting influence of God will pull soul awareness through the
layers of mind and Self-realization is experienced. The secret
to success in meditation is devoted and surrendered practice
on a regular schedule.

The Soul's Evolutionary
Status According to Awareness

The five degrees or conditions of the soul, while it is identified with the gross, subtle and fine aspects of creation, are:
dark, propelled, steady, devoted, and pure. It is therefore easy
for a person to determine his present status relative to his
ability to comprehend the true nature of Consciousness, and
to know what to do to improve in the direction of higher
understanding. Even a little effort in the right direction results
in soul awakening. Levels of soul awareness are also related to
the seven chakras, the subtle centers in the cerebro-spinal
system through which prana descends and ascends.

First Level — Due to the soul's almost complete involvement with matter at this level, it is only able to perceive the
gross sphere of material creation. At this level a person lives
in a "dark age" consciousness and must believe in the objective
world only, since he is not able to perceive or comprehend
anything else.

Second Level — Here, still somewhat attached to the material realm, one begins to awaken and faintly perceive the
existence of subtle forces in himself and in nature. His intellect is not yet refined but he is able to function more effec-

tively and to some degree use his executive abilities to further his purposes.

Third Level —Still somewhat deluded and attached to matter, one feels propelled to seek knowledge and begins to study the esoteric sciences. Because of increased ability to comprehend more subtle matters, one may partially understand the nature and character of cosmic mind and learn to relate to it in order to improve executive abilities and somewhat master the laws of causation and in this way begin to determine his destiny. If egoism is dominant, however, the use of subtle knowledge may cause further involvement with matter. To avoid this, one's motives in using one's creative abilities must be selfless.

Fourth Level —Here, because of awakened intuition and increased intellectual ability, one stands at the "door" between the outer and inner realms. There may be conflicting pulls between the realms so that one wavers, feeling strongly attracted to divine knowledge, but also feeling strongly attracted by the pull of the senses. It is at this level that one may make a commitment to the path of discipleship and be led to an enlightenment teaching, or to a personal relationship with a guru who is established in God-consciousness.

Fifth Level — As the result of the force of evolution or his own concentrated practice, one becomes able to comprehend the fine electric realms during meditation. Aum is spontaneously heard and the inner light manifests. After faithful adherence to spiritual practices one is lifted, by grace, into the realm connecting maya and Spirit. Here one literally "overcomes the world" by seeing through the fabric of nature and understanding how the creation drama occurs. One is then a true spiritual master, having awakened completely. He is a *siddha*, a perfected being. Living in this world or dwelling in subtle spheres the soul is ever free, and it is able to serve other seeking souls as a true Self-realized guru.

Sixth Level — After shedding all traces of karma and having fulfilled all duties, the soul rests in the awareness of being, on the "other side" of creation. The soul knows itself to be the boundless field of pure consciousness, as well as a wave on it. There remains a sense of individual existence but no delusion is present, nor can there ever be. Should such a being again incarnate, in causal, astral or gross spheres, it would do so only because of the impulse of God to be involved for the purpose of awakening souls and nourishing the universe.

Seventh Level — When the sense of individuality dissolves, only the field of pure consciousness remains. This is *nirvana*, the extinguishing of the flame of seeming individual light. The ray has been withdrawn into the light; the wave has receded into the ocean.

When an aspirant is steady in his resolve at the fourth level, he is drawn naturally to the fifth level. Here, his devotion causes him to surrender to higher influences and his nature is purified. With the purification of the mental field the intellect becomes unveiled and intuition fully awakens. It is then that the inner spiritual realms can be perceived and experienced.

At the first four levels one may experience shifts in awareness due to soul aspiration, the force of evolution, and the tendencies of the mind. Even a materialist may experience occasions of divine perception, while awake or during dreams, and a novice on the spiritual path may sometimes feel strongly inclined to indulge the senses. It is only at the fourth level and beyond, when sufficient awakening has occurred, that one is certain that he will never again become forgetful of spiritual matters.

Many newly awakened persons mistakenly assume that early breakthroughs are evidence of major advancement. They may then be inclined to settle for where they are in understanding, thinking that they are enlightened and, perhaps, becoming compulsive in their efforts to "enlighten" others. They do not know that they are but newly born, in the spiritual sense, and that they must allow themselves time to unfold to maturity.

I have seen much of this over the past several decades— Yoga "teachers" who themselves are not yet grounded in yogic practices; New Age "representatives" who wouldn't recognize the New Age if they were living in it; sincere but misguided authors who are almost completely lacking in discernment. Then, too, there are those given to illusory perceptions, even hallucinations, who feel themselves to be divine incarnations. One can, of course, teach others from his own level of understanding, but we should not presume to teach beyond our present understanding.

As the soul awakens in the direction of supreme realization, discernible stages are experienced. Turning from gross material manifestation one discerns the inner realm of subtle electric forces. He is able to discern the electricities within his own body and, if he is resolved on the spiritual path, he can begin to practice certain meditation exercises designed to increase this awareness. Before this he is not even able to understand the reason for such practice, much less be able to practice with any degree of effectiveness. The person who is even partially awake to the existence of internal forces, in his body and in nature, is suited to live in today's awakening world with understanding, because this is the time cycle during which powerful evolutionary forces are working in nature and in which millions of souls are awakening to participate in the process.

Awakening yet further, one becomes aware of the realm of magnetic attributes, their electricities and poles, and he is able to work with these fine forces in matter in constructive ways. The majority of the planet's population will comprehend this sphere several thousand years from now, even though a few are somewhat able to understand it now.

Awakening yet more the soul becomes aware of the realm beyond the veil of creation. This will be the common experience of many in the next true Age of Enlightenment many thousands of years hence.

The inner journey experienced during meditation has been described by many seers through the ages. We have a vivid description in the Holy Bible. The testimony of John, the beloved disciple of Jesus, is written in The Revelation of St. John the Divine, the last book in the New Testament.

I was in the Spirit on the Lord's day, and heard behind me a great voice, as of a trumpet. (1:10)

Being caught up in meditation, while communing with God, John inwardly discerned the sound of Aum *behind* his natural sense of hearing.

> And I turned to see the voice that spake with me. And being turned, I saw seven golden candlesticks. And in the midst of the seven candlesticks one like unto the Son of Man, clothed with a garment down to the foot, and girt about the breasts with a golden girdle. His head and his hairs were white like wool, as white as snow, and his eyes were as a flame of fire. And his feet like unto fine brass, as if they burned in a furnace; and his voice as the sound of many waters. And he had in his right hand seven stars; and out of his mouth went a sharp two-edged sword: and his countenance was as the sun shineth in his strength. And when I saw him, I fell at his feet as dead. And he laid his right hand upon me, saying unto me, Fear not; I am the first and the last: I am he that dieth, and was dead, and behold, I am alive for evermore, Amen; and have the keys to hell and death. (1:12—18)

This account corresponds exactly with descriptions of inner perception found in many yogic texts, as well as other sacred literature of the world. Upon hearing the primal sound of Aum during meditation, one turns to it and surrenders to it. The meditator's awareness is then drawn to the perception of the astral body, with the seven shining chakras. He may even perceive his astral body as separate from himself, which it is, just as the physical body is not really a part of us either. The aura of the astral form is like an enfolding garment, a radiation from the form, sometimes perceived as golden light. The astral brain, the crown chakra, is radiant white, and the spiritual eye is the flaming fire. The spiritual eye, when seen during meditation, is the door to inner realms. In this instance, St. John seems to have been observing his astral body from an objective point of view, much as it is possible to view the body objectively when one has left it for one reason or another. Ordinarily, when a meditator is undergoing early internal states, he perceives the spiritual eye as a result of ascending currents merging at the medulla oblongata. It is here in the body that dual currents emanate and flow into the upper brain as the result of an infusion of soul force.

> The mystery of the seven stars, which thou sawest in my right hand, and the seven golden candlesticks. The seven stars are the angels of the seven churches, and the seven candlesticks which thou sawest are the seven churches. (1:20)

The *angels* are the controlling life currents which flow through the chakras to sustain the astral and physical bodies. The chakras are non-material, being astral in nature and part of the subtle form. They are located in proximity to: the upper brain (crown chakra); the medulla oblongata (the positive pole of which is the spiritual eye); the cervical area; the thoracic area; lumbar area; sacrum; and base of the spine. Because of the different frequencies of life force manifesting through the respective chakras, different colored lights and different sounds emanate from them. These can be seen and heard during deep meditation. The "sound of many waters" is the commingling of astral frequencies emanating from the chakras. Contemplating what is behind the initial sounds that are heard, one experiences revelation.

> After this I looked, and, behold, a door was opened in heaven: and the first voice which I heard was as it were of a trumpet talking with me; which, said, Come up hither, and I will show thee things which must be hereafter. And immediately I was in the spirit: and, behold, a throne was set in heaven, and one sat on the throne. And he that sat was to look upon like a jasper and a sardine stone: and there was a rainbow round about the throne, in sight like unto an emerald. And round about the throne were four and twenty seats: and upon the seats I saw four and twenty elders sitting,

clothed in white raiment; and they had on their heads crowns of gold. And out of the throne proceeded lightnings and thunderings and voices: and there were seven lamps of fire burning before the throne, which are the seven Spirits of God. And before the throne there was a sea of glass like unto crystal: and in the midst of the throne and round about the throne, were four beasts full of eyes before and behind. (4:1-6)

Passing beyond the levels of material creation, St. John moved in awareness through the *door*, being summoned by the magnetic attracting force of the Godhead, and hearing the Aum sound continuously. In his awareness of individualization of Spirit he perceived the inner workings of the Godhead. Beholding the true source, he also perceived the outward-flowing force manifesting as the twenty-four active principles which make creation possible. These include: the twenty electricities (making possible the appearance of organs of perception, organs of action, subtle-element influences, and the five divisions of prana which regulate assimilating, eliminating, crystalizing, metabolizing and circulating functions throughout the universe), plus consciousness-feeling, ego, intelligence and mind.

He also perceived the seven divisions of divine influence in creation as the "spirits before the throne." He comprehended the nature of fine primal substance, maya, and the four aspects ("beasts" because they bar the soul from direct knowledge) comprising it: the creative force itself, fine particles, space, and time. The Son of Man is the "offspring" of nature. The Son of God is man's original condition. Once we are settled in meditative realization we inwardly comprehend the totality of Consciousness. The astral body of man has been described in religious literature as a "sealed casket" of knowledge. The seals (the chakras), when ascended, are the connecting portals to inner realms of consciousness.

PART THREE

Health,
Healing &
Radiant Living

ONE

Ayurveda: Science of Righteous Living and Longevity

There is a creative power nourishing the universe and we can learn to cooperate with it. Cooperating with this creative power is the way to mental, emotional and physical wellness and radiant living. What is here shared is a revival of knowledge, long known to adepts of the science of Ayurveda and now explained in terms easy for New Era man to understand.

The laws of nature are easy to comprehend; understanding them requires only that we observe them, consciously and willingly. This means that each person is responsible for his or her own wellness and harmony with these laws. The advice of qualified specialists may be sought from time to time if one requires help in removing the causes of distress which have manifested as the result of lack of harmony with natural laws, but by understanding the underlying causes of ill health it is possible for one to encourage nature's healing processes in oneself, avoid future discomfort and maintain radiant health of mind and body.

It is no accident that the trend of modern medicine is in the direction of self-responsibility on the part of the patient-client and that the total view of spirit-mind-body and environment is being increasingly examined and discussed. Since we are living during a time cycle when soul awareness is rapidly unfolding, it is only natural that a more cosmic view of matters be considered.

Introduction to Ayurveda,
Its History and Value

A truly holistic approach to wellness, righteous living and
longevity for the purpose of fulfilling destiny is the science
known as Ayurveda. The Sanskrit word is comprised of *ayus*,
life, and *veda*, knowledge. Ayurveda, then, is the "knowledge
of life," revealed to seers in times past, researched and verified
since then, and presenting a scientific approach which invites
our careful study and consideration.

Ayurveda can be traced back to at least 4000 B.C.; ref-
erences to it are found in the *Rig Veda*, the oldest body of
religious-philosophical scripture of which we have record on
the planet. The word *veda* means "to know," or knowledge.
The ancient compilations which are considered the four primary Vedas are the *Rig Veda, Sama Veda, Yajur Veda* and
Atharva Veda. Once believed to be a collection of history,
ritual and poetry, it is now realized that the Vedas contain
the essence of truth about how Consciousness expresses. Because they are the result of revelation, they can only be fully
comprehended from an enlightened state of consciousness.
Those not enlightened must be content to study commentaries written or explained by enlightened persons.

These four major texts of the Vedas were organized and
compiled into written form by a saintly person known to history as Vyasadeva, a term used to designate the common
understanding that he was but the one who brought the
existing data together. The Ayurveda is a subordinate scripture in which the theme of health, medicine, longevity and
fulfilled living is emphasized. Included in the category of medicine are the branches covering general medicine; major sur-
gery; ear, nose, eye, throat and mouth diseases; psychiatry;
pediatrics; toxicology; rejuvenation; and aphrodisiacs (vitalizing procedures).

It is important to remember that Ayurveda is based on an
understanding of the entire nature of Consciousness; it is thus
concerned not only with assisting man in the direction of total
wellness and function, but also with ensuring his conscious
cooperation with and participation in evolutionary processes

which can result in his becoming a cosmic-conscious being. The emphasis is *samhita*, true wholeness or completeness. While, for practical purposes, Ayurvedic regimens are useful to the average person who merely desires comfortable function, the ideal is to encourage the receptive person to unfold his innate capacities and eventually experience liberation of consciousness.

Translations of Ayurvedic texts have been published in several languages over the centuries. Two of the better known texts are the *Charaka Samhita* and *Sushruta Samhita*, the former dealing with general procedures and the latter with surgical ones. It is now believed that Ayurvedic knowledge flowed from India along trade routes to Arabia, Greece, Egypt, and later to Europe. It is also known to have flowed through Tibet and into all of Asia. It is a matter of historical record, for instance, that Hippocrates, the Greek physician who lived in the fourth century B.C. and who is known as "the father of Western medicine," visited India, as did some Greek philosophers of that era.

In India, general knowledge and practice of Ayurveda declined during the Dark Age, due to neglect and to the lack of interest of various invading cultures. Knowledge of this science is now again emerging on the world scene due to the interest and practical efforts of thoughtful persons.

During the eighth decade of our present century English translations of Ayurvedic texts began to become more prominantly available in Europe and America, and Ayurvedic clinics were established in a few major cities, staffed by medical doctors and physicians trained in Ayurvedic theory and practice. Credit for this spread of knowledge must be given to several generous persons, among them Dr. Vasant Lad, Dr. Chandrashekhar G. Thakkur, and the co-workers of Maharishi Mahesh Yogi. The Maharishi has been responsible, through his various research centers and educational institutions, for encouraging research and testing of Ayurvedic principles.

A verse from the *Charaka Samhita* reads, "All suffering which affects the mind or the body has ignorance for its cause, and all happiness has its basis in clear scientific knowledge."

A verse from the *Sushruta Samhita* reads, "This science of life is everlasting and bestows merit, prestige, happiness, longevity, livelihood, and heaven." Clearly, this approach to wellness is all-embracing and grounded in an understanding of the full range of the nature of Consciousness.

The Ayurvedic approach is researched, prevention-oriented, in most instances easily applied, free from harmful side-effects, economical, and aimed at treating the underlying causes of discomfort and disease, rather than merely suppressing symptoms. Pandit Shiv Sharma, a noted Ayurvedic physician, has stated, "In this approach the physician is more interested in knowing what kind of patient has a disease, than he is in knowing which disease the patient has." The ideal is to first understand the basic constitution of the patient-client and then be able to prescribe in line with exactly what he needs to have balance restored to mind and body.

To be successful in approach and application of this science one must have an understanding of the fundamental nature of the universe and its principles and laws. Health, it is taught, is the natural condition of a person who is living in perfect harmony with cosmic forces. When this prevails, all internal systems remain in balance. Disease, it then follows, is the result of being in disharmony with nature's forces and in suffering subsequent disequilibrium of internal forces and principles within the mind and body.

Because nature's principles are universal, all living things can be examined and their internal conditions understood by a knowledgeable person who is versed in this science of life and living. Four major complementary approaches can be taken to assist a person in the direction of wellness:

1. *The Cultivation of God-Consciousness* —For complete benefits one should understand the importance of attending to all duties of life with a constructive attitude. One should also understand the importance of spiritual practices, including the practice of regular meditation for the purpose of experiencing increasing levels of God-consciousness. Just as the God-head, through cosmic mind, is superior to the workings of the universe, so the soul, through mind, is superior to the workings

of the body. Therefore, when one experiences superconsciousness there is a natural and easy flow of superior forces through the mind and body. One then spontaneously thinks, feels and behaves in accord with the order of the universe, with the way of righteousness. As a result, stress will be absent from the body and internal processes will continue in perfect harmony and balance. Radiant health will be experienced and no discomfort or disease will manifest because no underlying causes for it can form.

2. *The Removal of Personal and Environmental Stress* — While internal stress is reduced as a result of meditation and orderly living, one is also advised to make whatever changes may be necessary in the living environment for the purpose of eliminating possible causes of stress which might lead to various internal conflicts. To this end one is advised to intelligently work with others in one's environment, to see to their education and to their total wellness. While the ordering of one's personal environment is something which can be accomplished rather easily, assisting in the ordering of the extended world environment may require greater vision and more involvement to implement desired ends. With the increase in the number of individuals who are fully healthy and functional, the general health and function of society dramatically improves.

3. *Behavior Modification* — Guidelines are given for diet, personal hygiene, exercise, and other life-enhancing procedures, as well as for daily and seasonal routines which restore inner balance and contribute to harmonizing of biological rhythms. While it is understood that one who is somewhat enlightened will easily live in accord with natural laws, persons who are not yet spiritually awakened often require guidance in basic matters relative to health and function. It is taught that through behavior modification and nutrition one can adapt to cosmic forces and resist environmental challenges which might occur from time to time.

4. *Specific Regimens* — These include cleansing procedures, dietary recommendations, and whatever else may be necessary to restore one to spiritual, psychological and physi-

cal health. Prescribed may be counseling, emotional release, massage (dry and with oils), the use of herbal substances, and the strengthening of the immune system by administering known rejuvenation procedures.

An Ayurvedic physician begins by carefully and fully examining the patient-client in order to arrive at an understanding of his basic constitution and to diagnose his problems. Included in the examination is a thorough questioning of the patient-client to hear his point of view and to obtain background information. Then follows physical examination, including careful examination of the pulse, which has long been an important aspect of Ayurvedic diagnostic procedures. The examining physician can also, by inference, learn much about the patient-client. No symptom, not even a vague complaint, is considered to be unimportant. Even attitudes, feelings and firm beliefs are considered to be essential to the final conclusions arrived at by the physician. Mild neurotic tendencies are quite possibly evidence of inner imbalance which can, sooner or later, contribute to subtle impulses which may change body chemistry and interfere with internal balance.

Health and long life are important to any person who desires to fulfill personal obligations and soul purposes. While one may fulfill personal obligations and purposes even while burdened with problems and ailments of various kinds, it is obvious that a more healthy, creative and successful life will be experienced when one is open to the universe and rid of restrictions. The ideal is to be responsive to the Holy Spirit, the all-pervading life of God, and to let it be gloriously expressed through a fully functional mind and body during one's present sojourn in the material realm.

The Governing Principles
Which Regulate Internal Processes

In the Ayurvedic approach to total health the influences of certain *governing principles* are essential to the understanding of why various therapeutic recommendations are made. If you have carefully studied the earlier sections of this book you will now more easily comprehend the following explanations about the governing principles of nature. The three major governing principle influences are *Water, Fire* and *Air.* In Ayurvedic literature these are referred to, respectively, as *kapha, pitta,* and *vata.* These governing principles are not actually the elements themselves, but the *influences* of the material causes of them. To explain further: Water governing principle is a combination of water and earth, with water predominating; Fire is a combination of fire and water, with fire predominating; and Air is a combination of air and ether, with air predominating. This should be remembered when Water, Fire and Air governing principle influences are referred to hereafter in this text. Too, all of the element influences are present in some degree in any one element influence or governing principle, with the named influence being the major one.

These governing principles are present in all the forms abounding in nature, including the foods we eat. Because of this, anything in nature can be prescribed as a therapeutic agent if its specific qualities are known and if it is administered correctly.

In this system it is taught that each person is born with a basic constitution, a basic characteristic psychosomatic nature resulting from element influences contributed by one's parents and modified by environmental circumstances. This is why we are all different, as embodied beings. The ideal would be to have all three governing principles, those of Water, Fire and Air, in balance, but this is almost never the case. However, to contribute to the development of this ideal state of balance one can meditate, cultivate constructive thinking habits, remain calm and emotionally balanced, adjust personal behavior, attend to specific dietary plans, and do anything else which is useful to this purpose. In other words, we need not feel restricted or victimized if our basic constitution is in need of balancing.

When one or more governing principles are aggravated, or increased in influence to a point where major disharmony and imbalance prevail, one may be inclined to experience changes in mood, behavior or physical function. Likewise, if certain governing principles are suppressed, disharmony will also result. It is within range of available therapeutic strategies to bring about harmony among the three governing principles which prevail in mind and body

The following information will be of help in understanding the influences of the three governing principles:

1. *Water-Element Influences* — Bodily stability, energy, lubrication, unctuousness (oily/greasy). Psychological effects are attachment, tendency to accumulate, and willingness to forgive others. This governing principle is aggravated by lack of physical exercise, sedentary habits, eating of too many sweet, acid, salty and oily foods, or too much milk, sugar, fat and sweet fruits. Heaviness, drowsiness, itching of skin and constipation can result.

2. *Fire-Element Influences* — Body heat, internal body temperature, digestion, power of perception (eyesight). The psychological effects are understanding, intelligence, anger, hate, jealousy. This governing principle is aggravated by fear, anger, grief, too much physical exercise, incomplete digestion and eating too many foods which are bitter, acid, salty and dry. Hyperacidity, fainting, perspiration, excessive thirst, paleness of skin, and delirium can result.

3. *Air-Element Influences* —Movement, breathing, natural urges to eliminate waste products, tissue transformation, sensory functions. This governing principle is aggravated by excesses of any kind, grief, anxiety, fear, strain or stress of any kind, suppression of natural urges, and hard falls or serious accidents. Stiffness, rough skin, shivering, hoarseness of voice, yawning, dryness, thirst and sad moods can result. A sense of fear, emptiness and general anxiety may be characteristics of a person in whom the Air governing principle is very strong.

Since the governing principles pervade all of nature, including the body, when they are in balance perfect health and function are automatically experienced. When they are not in harmony, disorder tends to follow. Air governing principle influences the movements of prana, life force, in the body, and disturbances of the Air governing principle can upset the equilibrium of prana flows. The practice of certain pranayamas can assist in maintaining the balance of the Air governing principle.

Psychological conditions can change the balance of the governing principles in the body. Strong emotions, positive or negative, contribute to either health and function or disease and premature death. Firm beliefs and emotional states can contribute to actual changes in body chemistry, which changes can be beneficial or detrimental, depending upon their character. The intentional cultivation of optimism, faith and happiness strengthens the immune system and causes all body functions to improve. Habits of pessimism, fear, grief, depression and a feeling of alienation from life can weaken the immune system and impair body function.

When symptoms are recognizable they are but evidence of deeper causes which have been present at subtle levels for a much longer period of time. The purpose of Ayurvedic therapies is not only to eliminate symptoms but also to remove the underlying subtle causes so that problems will not arise again. When a person is self-responsible for his own wellness he will be able to maintain a life style which will encourage permanent wellness at all times. The Ayurvedic physician prescribes and gives emotional support, but the patient-client is the one responsible for final results in his life.

Except for harmful influences which are introduced into the body, diseases arise from within as the result of internal disturbance. The body's immune system is quite capable of resisting the intrusion of viruses and other potentially threatening agents if one is healthy and the governing principles are in balance. In fact, one of the key purposes of Ayurvedic regimens is to ensure a strong immune system and to encourage the internal "fires" which are capable of metabolizing foods and transforming them into needed substances.

When internal fire (*agni*) is weak the processes of digestion, metabolism and nutrient transformation are impaired. Toxins accumulate which clog the systems and interfere with function, weakening the various body systems. Purification procedures may be prescribed for the purpose of removing toxic buildup so that health can be restored. Daily elimination of normal waste products is encouraged as routine. The three major waste products are feces, urine and perspiration. These products are not totally waste; they are in fact essential to function and are part of the food transformation cycle.

For instance, feces supply nutrients through intestinal tissues before being eliminated as waste. They also maintain strength and tone in the large intestine. The urinary system removes salt, water and urea (nitrogenous waste) from the body. Urine is produced in the large intestine and helps to maintain the balance of water electrolytes (electrical conductors) within the body fluids. Normal urine production is essential to maintaining normal blood pressure and volume. If urine production is scanty it may be because water is being retained in the tissues of the body. Perspiration helps maintain body temperature, carries off wastes (as does urine), keeps the skin pores healthy and is beneficial to the skin in that it promotes smoothness and elasticity. Perspiration massaged into the skin and allowed to dry, before bathing, cleanses and softens the skin.

The Seven Tissues
of the Physical Body

Seven tissues, the results of food transformation, comprise the *dhatus*, the "constructing elements" of the body. They maintain the functions of the different organs, systems and vital parts. They are also a part of the protective mechanisms of the body. All of them are the result of inner fire, the transforming influence, fulfilling its purposes. In sequence, these tissues are:

1. *Plasma* — Contains nutrients; transports them throughout the body to build and maintain organs and systems. In women, appears as breast milk and menstrual fluid.

2. *Blood* — Carries nutrients and oxygen (also prana from oxygen) and transports carbon dioxide from the inner parts of the body to the lungs, there to be exhaled.

3. *Muscle* — Covers some organs and provides movement to joints so that functions can be performed.

4. *Fat* — Maintains lubrication and provides insulation against a cold environment.

5. *Bone* — Supports the body structure.

6. *Marrow* — Soft, fat vascular tissue inside the bones. Nerve tissue is of a similar tissue characteristic and carries motor and sensory impulses.

7. *Reproductive Tissue* — The end result of nutrient transformation; it makes possible reproduction of the species.

If any of these supporting tissues is deficient, the ones following will suffer. For radiant health, it is important that the transformative fires be strong and that all governing principles remain balanced. The final result after the seven successive stages have been completed is the life essence (*ojas*) itself. This fine essence imparts radiance to the body, brilliance to the mind, and magnetism to the personality. An inner light emanates into the environment and shines for others to see. It is also accumulated in the body as a result of meditation, calmness, pure thinking and purposeful living. It is wasted through excessive talk, restlessness, stress, dissipation of any kind, and poor health habits.

The Universe is Within
Us, as Well as Around Us

What occurs in the cosmos occurs in the body of man— the universe is within us as well as around us. There is no retaining surface, in body or mind, where we leave off and the larger world begins. Our bodies are formed of the same substance of which the cosmos is formed, and the same governing principles and forces flow through everything. This is why perfect internal balance is only possible when we are in harmony with all of the forces and expressions of nature. By understanding our own internal processes we can more easily understand the processes of our larger, cosmic body.

The ideal of Ayurveda is to offer man the opportunity to unfold his inborn capacities and experience perfect unity with all life. It is, then, more than a system of wellness and function; Ayurveda embraces all of the procedures which can allow the soul to experience true freedom.

TWO

Determining Your Basic
Psychosomatic Constitution

Every person is born with a basic psychosomatic constitution which remains generally the same throughout his life. The Greek word *psyche* means soul, but it is often defined in the West as spirit, soul or mind, with mind being the commonly accepted definition. *Somatic* refers to the physical body.

Because of variables, no two people are identical so far as their psychosomatic constitution is concerned. In relationship to the three governing principles, a person may possess one of several possible governing principle constitutions, depending upon the dominant influences and the possible combinations. One may be predominantly Water, Fire or Air, or: Water-Fire, Water-Air, Fire-Water, Fire-Air, Air-Water, Air-Fire or Water-Fire-Air. These ten constitutional types will vary because of the percentage of mixtures of governing influences.

Governing principle influences are determined at conception, due to the combined characteristics of the parents, their environmental circumstances, time and circumstances of intercourse, circumstances surrounding the mother during the gestation period, the mother's spiritual and psychological state, and the food she eats. The soul also brings constitutional characteristics with it from the astral realm, and these also contribute to the final result. We see, then, how intricate the process of determining individual constitutional types can be.

We cannot do anything about what we were provided with

at birth, so far as our basic psychosomatic constitution is concerned, but we can do something about the matter once we
are sufficiently informed and determined to make changes in
the direction of balance.

The Influences of the Three
Gunas and Spiritual Awareness

Since the three gunas—sattva, rajas and tamas—are present
in all of nature, they influence mind and body. The degree of
individual spiritual awareness is also influential; one's constitutional nature is not static but, because of various internal
and external forces, is constantly being modified.

Sattva guna tends to contribute to order in mind and body,
and to influence function in the direction of harmony. Rajas
guna tends to contribute to action, to motion and change.
Tamas guna contributes to inertia and non-change. The cultivation of sattvic tendencies, then, is useful to higher purposes.

Because of the intimate interrelationship between mind
and body, the body being considered an extension of the
mind, what occurs in the mind influences body function and
what occurs in the body tends to influence mental states. It
therefore follows that the cultivation of constructive mental
states is useful if one desires to express through a healthy and
functional body.

Superior soul awareness virtually assures a healthy mental
condition which, in turn, will reflect in body function. A person who is spiritually aware is naturally inclined to always
think correctly and to do spontaneously those things which
will ensure health of body and harmony with the environment.

The degree of ability to comprehend, and the outlook on
life one maintains, are both strongly influenced by the three
gunas, or attributes of nature. In the Bhagavad Gita (17:1-13),
we read:

> The faith of people is threefold, according to their
> basic nature. Man's evolutionary status corresponds
> to his state of consciousness and mental states. Rightly
> resolved but partially deluded people worship the

gods, restless and still more deluded people worship the demigods, and completely deluded people worship the spirits of friends and relatives and spirits. Extremely materialistic people with religious impulses perform self-punishing austerities, injure themselves and suppress the workings of Spirit. By the foods we take into the body, and by our manner of giving, the level of understanding can be determined. Those who are on the upward way love foods which promote life, vitality, strength, health, joy and cheerfulness. Restless people are drawn to partake of foods which are bitter, sour, overly seasoned and which are hard on the system. Lower types eat tasteless, stale and unclean foods. High-minded people give according to scriptural law, without any expectation whatever of reward. They give wisely because they feel it to be their duty to make right use of the substance of the world. Restless, selfish people give for the sake of expected reward, and for the sake of personal recognition. The lower types give grudgingly, if at all, without faith, and they tend to try to get things for nothing, without making just compensation.

These simple guidelines offer us the opportunity to see ourselves as we presently are and to decide to make useful changes if change is in order. Finally, Krishna shares helpful advice (17:14-19):

Discipline of the body is said to include reverence for the spiritual teacher, pure intentions, cleanliness, control of vital forces, and harmlessness. Discipline of speech includes the effort to speak kindly, and to be truthful. Discipline of the mind includes silence at appropriate times, self-control, and high resolve. This is all to be observed without any expectation of reward. Whatever we do in order to gain name or fame is a waste of time and effort and is not of lasting value. Harming ourselves or others is destructive and such behavior is due to ignorance.

That we can, by commitment and discipline, be intentionally involved with our spiritual unfoldment is clearly stated in all of the great world scriptures. Heaviness and darkness can be dissolved from the mind as the result of wise behavior, and restlessness can be neutralized as the result of cultivating the moral qualities and experiencing Self-realization.

A Simple Self-Examination for Determining the Basic Constitution

When taking this examination, consider the characteristics in relationship to your life cycle from earliest memory to the present time, since certain presently existing characteristics may be due to minor changes recently experienced. Do not think of any characteristic as good or bad, but simply respond as honestly as you can. You may want to write the answers on a separate sheet of paper, unless you are using this text as a personal workbook.

Once you have determined your basic psychosomatic constitution, almost everything else you read in this section will be more meaningful to you, because you will be able to relate the information given to your own situation.

If two or three answers seem to you to be almost equally true, select the one which is most accurate. Bear in mind that for a thorough determination it will be useful to be examined by a qualified Ayurvedic specialist, who may be able to discern things about you that you cannot see for yourself. This is but a general self-test and will provide basic information useful to you in your attempt to better understand yourself.

Ways in Which Governing Principles are Modified

Governing principles are balanced in the system by our state of consciousness, the thoughts we think, the emotions we express, the foods we eat and the environment we regulate. They are forces which are subject to modification, so we need not think in terms of our present constitutional nature being fixed or unchangeable; it can be somewhat altered in favor of

Characteristic	Water	Fire	Air
1. Body	( ) Broad shoulders, hips	( ) Moderate	( ) Narrow shoulders, hips
2. Weight	( ) Heavy	( ) Medium	( ) Thin (tendons show)
3. Endurance; strength	( ) Good	( ) Fair	( ) Poor
4. Skin	( ) Oily, pale, moist, white	( ) Soft, fair, oily, delicate, pink to red	( ) Dry, rough, cool, darker
5. Skin Aging	( ) Smooth, few wrinkles	( ) Freckles, moles, pigmentation	( ) Dry, flaky, wrinkles
6. Hair	( ) Oily	( ) Medium	( ) Dry
7. Hair color	( ) Medium blonde, medium to dark brown	( ) Light blonde, red, light brown	( ) Dark brown to black
8. Hair texture	( ) Straight or wavy, thick	( ) Wavy, fine, soft	( ) Curly, kinky
9. Digestion, appetite	( ) Moderate, no extreme hunger	( ) Sharp hunger	( ) Irregular or heavy diet but stays thin
10. Teeth	( ) White, large, little decay	( ) Yellowish, moderate size	( ) Large, protruding, crooked
11. Eyes	( ) Large, blue or brown	( ) Hazel, green, gray	( ) Small, black or brown
12. Elimination	( ) Heavy, slow, thick	( ) Soft, oily, loose	( ) Dry, hard, tendency to constipation
13. Sex Drive	( ) Cyclical, infrequent	( ) Moderate	( ) Frequent
14. Physical Activity	( ) Little or no exercise, lethargic	( ) Enjoys regular exercise	( ) Restless, active
15. Mental Activity	( ) Calm, steady	( ) Aggressive, intelligent	( ) Flighty, restless

	Water	Fire	Air
16. Voice, speech	( ) Low-pitched, melodious, slow, monotone	( ) Medium-pitched, sharp, laughing	( ) High-pitched, fast, dissonant, vibrato, weeping
17. Taste, food preferences	( ) Dry, light, low-fat, sweet, pungent	( ) Medium, light, sweet, warm, bitter, astringent	( ) Oily, heavy, sweet, soupy, salty, sour
18. Sleep pattern	( ) Deep, prolonged, easy	( ) Sound, medium	( ) Short, insomnia
19. Memory	( ) Long-term memory	( ) Good, not prolonged	( ) Short-term memory
20. Financial behavior	( ) Saves regularly	( ) Saves, but spends on luxuries	( ) Money quickly spent
21. Reaction to stress	( ) Indifferent, complacent, withdraws	( ) Angry, jealous, irritable	( ) Fearful, anxious
22. Dreams	( ) Water, ocean, river, lake, erotic	( ) Fire, war, violence, strife, anger	( ) Fearful, flying, running, jumping
23. Mental predisposition	( ) Stable, logical	( ) Judging, artistic	( ) Questions, theorizes
24. Resting radial pulse (quality)	( ) Slow, moves like a swan	( ) Moderate, jumps like a frog	( ) Thready, slithers like a snake
25. Radial resting pulse (number of beats per minute)	( ) 60–70	( ) 70–80	( ) 80–100 plus
	Subtotal *Water* _____ times 4= _____	Subtotal *Fire* _____ times 4= _____	Subtotal *Air* _____ times 4= _____

Approximate body type, based on highest subtotal: _____

a more harmonious condition, if such modification is required, by our own efforts in the right direction.

If, for any reason, the governing principles of Water, Fire or Air are upset, the symptoms of problems associated with each principle can be observed. These symptoms can be mild, medium or pronounced. If the imbalance is mild, only a little discomfort may be experienced. If medium, more discomfort would be experienced, and if the imbalance is pronounced, serious discomfort or a diseased condition might be obvious. The governing principles are subtle influences, but their effects are manifested in the mind and body.

An increase or aggravation of Air governing principle (the movement and circulating principle), might be ascertained by evidence of harshness of speech, emaciation, swarthiness of skin, throbbing of the limbs, desire for hot foods, insomnia, lack of vitality, constipation, tremors, impairment of the functions of the sense organs, giddiness, depression, roughness of the skin, sometimes loss of consciousness, atrophy of bone marrow, fear, anxiety and grief. With decrease of the Air governing principle the symptoms are diminished movement, depression, stupefaction, weakness of limbs; the patient-client is predisposed to diseases due to increase of the Water governing principle, such as anorexia, nausea, and variability of appetite.

When the Fire governing principle is increased it may cause desire for cold things, decreased sleep, loss of strength, weakness of the senses, fainting, yellow coloration of feces, urine and skin, excessive hunger, thirst, burning sensations, hyper-acidity, weakening of vital essence (*ojas*), and a bitter taste in the mouth. When this governing principle is decreased the symptoms may be sour stomach, anorexia, indigestion, tremors, heaviness, pallor of nails and eyes, increase of mucus, lack of body luster, stiffness, and irregular burning and pain sensations.

When the Water governing principle is increased, symptoms may include coldness, heaviness, depression, thick sensation in joints, dullness of appetite, cough, light-colored stools, a feeling of fullness of body, blocking of channels through which fluids and subtle forces flow, fainting, whiteness of skin and sleepiness. When decreased, symptoms may be dryness, absence of watery substances in usual places of the body except the stomach, thirst, giddiness, general debility, looseness of joints, wakefulness, tachycardia, dehydration, aching, burning, heat, trembling, and loss of consciousness.

The attending Ayurvedic physician would then be able to determine which governing principles were overly active or diminished in function and would then proceed accordingly to encourage balance between them.

Unless overly influenced by dietary and other factors, the governing principles are more usually influenced during different seasons because of the preponderance of the governing influences in nature. For instance, Air governing principle is accumulated during summer months, aggravated during rainy seasons and reduced in intensity during autumn. The Fire governing principle accumulates in influence during warm rainy seasons, is aggravated in autumn and is reduced in early winter. The Water governing principle is increased in early winter, aggravated in spring and is reduced during the summer months. Because seasonal changes may occur differently in different parts of the world, adaptation will have to be made when ascertaining them and their influence.

Usually, with an increase of any governing principle in the body, one feels inclined to avoid anything that might cause further increase and instead is led to do those things which would reduce the influence and increase the influence of the governing principles which are at the time naturally decreased in the body.

Therapeutic regimens prescribed to balance the governing principles would include any useful approach to meet the needs. These might include internal cleansing, massage (dry or with oils), rest or activity, psychological counseling, meditation, dietary routine and the use of herbs.

Ayurveda also includes the prescribing of minute dosages of certain herbs, metals and other substances, much as homeopathic remedies are administered by some physicians today. This is accomplished by reducing the principle ingredient, sometimes hundreds or thousands of times, until only the subtle essence of the original ingredient remains. This works at deeper levels, is non-toxic, and often results in remarkable benefits to the patient-client.

Also, in our current era, there are supplementary therapeutic procedures which might be useful, such as polarity therapy, acupressure, zone therapy during which pressure points on the feet are worked with, and chiropractic.

Chiropractic is the approach taken by the physician who uses his hands to adjust the skeletal structure of the body, usually the vertebral column, in order to remove nerve interference so that the natural flow of nerve force, and prana, can flow from the brain down through the spinal cord and out into the body to nourish body systems. Correct adjustments of the vertebrae assist in allowing the body to receive the full flow of nerve force. Posture is generally improved as the result of adjustments and an increased degree of well-being is experienced.

Regular practice of superconscious meditation aids greatly in balancing the governing principles of the body because of the infusion of fine but influential forces which flow into the brain, nervous system and body. Any therapeutic approach which proves helpful is useful, but it is the cosmic life force which is responsible for positive final results.

Flowing With the Rhythms of the Universe

When we can live in harmony with nature, our internal rhythms flow in accord with the rhythms of the universe. Since many people in industrialized societies do not always live in harmony with nature, it is well that we learn a little about how to do so to the best of our ability. The body has marvelous powers of adaptation, but it is useful for us to do the best we can to cooperate with nature's trends.

All of nature, including man, is influenced by the seasons due to the movement of Planet Earth around the sun. Nature is also influenced by the hours of sunlight and darkness, and the gravitational pull of the moon and sun, as well as the sun's reflected light from the moon.

During autumn, the Air governing principle is influential in nature and Air-related problems can occur in people in whom the Air governing principle is naturally pronounced. In winter the Water governing principle is influential in nature and Water-related problems can occur in people in whom the Water governing principle is pronounced, causing colds, respiratory difficulties and the like. During spring the Water governing principle gives way to Fire, and the accumulated Water conditions are reduced. During summer the Fire governing principle is influential in nature and Fire-related problems can occur in people in whom the Fire governing principle is pronounced.

One is therefore advised to do those things which will reduce the governing principles in the body which correspond to the seasons. In this way health and function can more easily be maintained. During autumn one would begin to change over from a summer dietary program to one more suitable for the winter months, making gradual changes as the new season approaches and progresses.

During winter one would eat foods which result in an increase of Fire and Air governing influences and during spring one would begin to change from a winter diet to one which is more suitable for summer, making the changes gradually as summer approaches. During winter, for instance, the diet would include foods that are heavier and heat-producing, while during summer the diet would include foods which are lighter and cooling, with more liquids and more fresh fruits and vegetables.

One would also dress appropriately for the different seasons—warmer during the colder months and lighter clothing during the warm seasons. Most of the obvious things come naturally to us, but our food choices do not always come so naturally, because of a tendency to eat what appeals to the senses but not necessarily what answers the body's inner needs.

During the day the governing principles are influential at regular intervals. From six to ten A.M., the Water governing principle is predominant. At this time the body is made ready for the day's activities and internal secretions, including the glandular secretions, are in motion due to the Air influence just prior to dawn. One may feel a little heavy, but with energy emerging. This is also the body's cleansing cycle, when waste products are eliminated, so this is the ideal time to attend to bathroom routines. Persons with a predominantly Water constitution may not want to eat breakfast, because this can increase the Water governing principle in the body.

From ten A.M. until two P.M. the Fire governing principle is strongest, and this is the ideal time to schedule the major meal of the day. Digestive fire is strong at this time. A short rest after the midday meal would be in order, if convenient.

From two to six P.M. the Air governing principle is influential, and one may feel lighter but beginning to tire from the day's activities. The early evening hours are a good time to relax and meditate, then have a light meal. A short walk would be useful after the evening meal.

From six P.M. until ten P.M., the Water governing principle is again influential and one would feel a natural inclination to eliminate body wastes and prepare for sleep.

From ten P.M. to two A.M., the Fire governing principle is again dominant; then the Air governing principle once more becomes influential, until six A.M.

These internal changes occur naturally, and are in harmony with the forces in nature. To arrange one's life, if possible, so that activities are scheduled in harmony with the natural environmental rhythms is extremely useful and contributes to health and function.

A Practical Way to Start the Day

The first thing upon awakening in the morning, breathe a prayer of thanksgiving and look forward to what is to unfold. If you have planned the day's activities the night before, you will be better able to begin the day with enthusiasm.

1. *Eliminate Body Wastes* — Evacuate the bowels and bladder and bathe the body, cleaning all body openings to remove accumulated matter. Ayurvedic texts recommend a body massage with warm sesame oil before bathing, including the head and the soles of the feet. This is believed to balance the Air governing principle in the body as well as clean and lubricate the skin.

2. *Oral Hygiene* — The mouth should be rinsed with water and the teeth and gums cleaned. Also recommended is scraping of the tongue with a smooth instrument such as a spoon, to remove accumulated matter. The tongue can also be massaged and the gums massaged with oil to stimulate circulation and strengthen the roots of the teeth.

3. *Variations* — You may want to practice a few rounds of the abdominal lift during the morning bathroom routine.

This will energize the body and awaken vital forces, strength-ening the gastric fire. Some also like to perform the nasal wash at this time, to encourage drainage from the sinus cavities in the head.

4. *Morning Meditation* — If *yogasanas* (hatha yoga pos-tures) are performed, this would be a natural time to do them, followed by mild pranayama and meditation for at least twen-ty minutes, or longer if desired.

It would be well to plan ahead and retire earlier at night in order to allow enough time for these morning routines.

Persons with predominantly Air and Fire constitutions may want to eat a light breakfast, although this is a matter of preference. One's feelings about the matter are the best guide.

Other Rhythms to Consider

Persons with a Water constitution may find that they have a tendency to retain fluids during the full moon phase. Many also notice that they become more easily emotionally aroused during this phase of the moon, and more introverted during the dark phase of the moon.

In all matters it is useful to be conscious of nature's rou-tine, which is measured in intervals of activity and rest. Periods of activity are for accomplishment, while periods of rest are for being restored, literally re-created.

Exercise Programs for the Basic Constitutions

Individuals with predominantly Water governing principle constitutions, because of their tendency to be comfortable with themselves, even complacent, often avoid any regular exercise. They are the very ones who should engage in a pro-gram of regular and sustained exercise, and who, once they are involved in such a program, will thrive on it.

Those with Fire governing principle constitutions may not have as much stamina, although they usually enjoy exer-cise. They should not overdo it, however, because their basic nature may cause them to be too competitive.

Those persons with Air governing principle constitutions may be too frantic in their exercise programs, because of their already restless and active natures. Frantic exercise would only aggravate the Air principle, causing them to be hyperactive and to tire themselves.

A good general rule is to avoid extremes while ensuring regular exercise in a manner which best suits the basic constitution. Especially with running, cycling, action sports such as tennis, basketball or other competitive sports, the pace should not be such that one becomes exhausted as a result of participation. A more useful approach is to exercise to the point of feeling comfortably exhilarated, with a sense of well-being and serene joy. Swimming, walking, hiking in the woods or low mountains, and any exercise performed at a comfortable pace would be ideal. Extremes should be avoided, as they overwork the systems of the body and interfere with the inner calm generated as a result of meditation and cultivation of the inner life.

Conscious Tai Chi Chuan practice is excellent. These meditative movements improve total awareness, body balance, concentration and the awakening and circulation of pranas.

Several times a week, exercise should be engaged in which is sufficiently vigorous to stimulate the cardiovascular system and force deeper breathing. This will maintain strength of the body, provide extra oxygen and cleanse the tissues of carbon dioxide and other accumulated waste products. After a cooling-down period a bath can be taken, followed by a short rest period.

Of special value is a regular routine of hatha yoga practice. While this does not come under the heading of vigorous exercise, the practice of various asanas and pranayamas will strengthen muscles, impart flexibility to the joints, improve glandular function, and stimulate the circulation of blood, lymph and other fluids throughout the body. The subtle pranas will also be beneficially influenced and dormant life force will be awakened.

While a more complete program may be learned and practiced, I include here a few of the basic procedures which one may include in a simple daily program. Hatha yoga should be experienced in a meditative mood during which one is relaxed and attuned to inner processes. In this way spiritual awareness is encouraged and one is more easily attuned to cosmic forces.

Hatha yoga practices are extemely beneficial. The ideal way to practice is while in a relaxed, meditative mood. Feel, as you flow through your routine, that you are open to the energies of the cosmos. Feel that your body processes are in harmony with the processes of nature. Do not struggle or strain. Assume the asana, hold for a comfortable duration, and flow out of it and relax. Conclude by lying flat on your back, being totally relaxed, contemplating yourself as one with the Infinite.

Include in your hatha yoga routine, or at another time, the practice of *uddiyana bandha*, the stomach lifting exercise. With practice this can be done several times while the breath is held out. In the *Hatha Yoga Pradipika* (2:54) we read, "Uddiyana is so called by the yogis because by its practice prana flows in the sushumna." This *mudra* (exercise for controlling prana) enlivens the entire system and strengthens the digestive fire, as well as awakening dormant vital forces throughout.

At some point during your routine, perhaps just before meditating, after a period of relaxation, practice alternate nostril breathing for a few minutes. Inhale through the right nostril, hold, exhale through the left nostril. Take deeper than usual breaths as you do this, but do not strain. Use the fingers of your right hand to close off the nostril not being used. This pranayama will balance the flows of force in the body and clear the mind for concentration.

Experience the Healing
Forces of Nature

Now and then, walk barefoot on the grass. This will energize the body and balance out its forces. Spend time by an ocean or a lake. Walk in the mountains. Experience the solitude of the desert. Swim when you can, in an open body of water, or in a swimming pool if a lake is not convenient. Feel yourself to be one with nature.

Daily, spend time out of doors to experience the normalizing effects of full spectrum light. Do not wear glasses of any kind during this time. Allow the light to flow through the eyes to nourish the glands and systems of the body. It has been discovered that artificial light, without the full range of the spectrum in it, can contribute to chemical changes in the body, and even disease. Even indoors, people become more cheerful and productive when full spectrum light sources are present, instead of light bulbs and tubes which are deficient in some of the colors of the spectrum. If sunglasses must be used from time to time, use only grey tinted lenses, not the various colored ones. The latter will prevent the complete range of color from entering through the eyes and optic nerves, and from thence to the brain and pituitary gland.

Listen to the wind, soar with the clouds, commune with living things and appreciate animals and all forms of life. You will find the universe to be your friend, benevolent and supportive. You will have no enemies and your timing will always be perfect.

Rabindranath Tagore, the great poet sage of India, wrote in *Gitanjali*:

When one knows thee, then alien there is none, then
no door is shut. Oh, grant me my prayer that I may never
lose the touch of the one in the play of the many.

FOUR

Food As Consciousness

Just as everything in the universe is a manifestation of the One Life, so food is Consciousness. The food we eat not only provides the carbohydrates, proteins, vitamins, minerals, enzymes and other necessary nutrients; it also provides life force, the influences of the three gunas (the electric attributes in nature), and the three governing principle influences which determine internal states.

Food selection and preparation, then, should be a conscious exercise because the end results will affect body, mind and spiritual awareness.

According to Ayurveda, how we acquire our food is important. If harvested, it should be collected with care and thankfulness. If purchased or received from another by whatever means, it should be obtained honestly and in a spirit of appreciation. Food which is dishonestly acquired, or paid for with resources which have been dishonestly accumulated, will not have as wholesome an effect upon mind or body. An attitude or feeling of dishonesty will taint the mind and emotional nature, resulting in less than ideal effects from the eating of food.

Fresh, live foods should be selected for personal use and for serving to family members or guests. Persons employed in a food service business, such as a produce store or a restaurant, should be aware that they are offering food as Consciousness to buyers and customers. In this way any transaction becomes a spiritual exercise which benefits both seller and buyer.

Food should be prepared in a clean, quiet environment. Everything involved in the process, from the state of consciousness of the person preparing the food to the utentils used in its preparation, should be sattvic, pure and elevating. One's hands should be washed well before beginning preparations. A sick or unwell person, or one who is angry, moody, or emotionally disturbed, should not prepare food for others.

In the Ayurvedic approach, even though foods are often recommended to meet the special needs of the different constitutional types, a wide variety of ingredients is available so that one will not need to be concerned that basic nutritional requirements will not be met. In most instances, foods from the basic groups can be easily utilized to please the most discerning palate as well as to satisfy nutritional needs. Because a variety of foods is available in this approach there is little concern about whether or not a balance of carbohydrates, proteins, vitamins and other nutrients is supplied. These nutrients will be naturally available in suitable quantities if a sensible approach is taken. The major emphasis is upon ensuring that the governing principles—Water, Fire and Air influences—are properly considered to meet individual needs.

The approach to this matter is unique to this system, in that it deals with the *tastes* of foods, because it is the taste which influences the governing principles in the body. This may seem a bit strange when first learned, but it will be better comprehended as we examine the origins of the various tastes. Six tastes are recommended at most meals, with the exception of special instances, with tastes provided in greater measure for specific purposes.

The six tastes found in foods are sweet, sour, salty, bitter, pungent, and astringent. They are derived from the governing principle element influences in the following ways:

The combination of Earth and Water in nature produces the sweet taste. The combination of Earth and Fire produces the sour taste. The combination of Water and Fire produces the salty taste. The combination of Air and Space produces the bitter taste. The combination of Earth and Air produces the astringent taste, and the combination of Fire and Air produces the pungent taste.

It is easy to see that foods containing the governing principles which correspond to the governing principles which influence the body will have their effects. For instance, sweet, sour and salty tastes will increase the Water governing principle and decrease Air. Pungent, bitter and astringent tastes will increase Air and decrease Water. Pungent and salty tastes will increase Fire. Sweet, bitter and astringent tastes will decrease Fire. Simply put, if the governing principle is present in foods according to their tastes, they will increase that influence in the body. If they are absent that influence in the body will be decreased. This is an easy way to select foods for the purpose of contributing to the balancing of the governing principles of the body, and such body influences will also affect the mental and emotional states.

Charts listing foods and their governing principle influences according to taste effects are included in this chapter. The chapter following provides sample menus and food routines for specific purposes.

More Guidelines to
Food Selection and Use

Food qualities are also classified as heavy or oily (and moist), light or dry, and hot or cold in temperature. As a general rule heavy, oily foods increase the Water governing principle in the body and decrease Air. Light, dry foods increase Air and decrease Water. Hot or cold foods, respectively, increase or decrease Fire.

Water should not be taken in large quantities for about one hour before or after a meal, because it tends to dilute the digestive juices. Water before a meal may cause one to lose weight and water after a meal may cause one to gain weight. Milk and soups can be taken with the meal, and small quantitites of fluid if the food is too dry.

Honey, if used as a sweetener, should not be used in excess and always in its natural state, not heated, because heating destroys the nutrient value. Honey should not be used with equal amounts of butter, although in some recipes honey and butter are used, but with less honey in volume compared to the butter. Honey, milk, and butter in the form of *ghee* (clarified butter) is sometimes recommended with herbal remedies because herbal influences are carried more deeply into the system when they are added.

The amount of food eaten at any one meal should be moderate. The general advice is to fill the stomach only about one-third full, perhaps the amount of food which would fill the cupped hands, but this is merely a statement to give a general idea. The better way is to eat in a relaxed mood, chewing the food well to assist digestion, and eating only until you feel comfortable and light.

By following a well-balanced dietary plan one will have no difficulty in providing the body with all essential nutrients using this approach to food selection and eating. If special needs arise these can be met easily, and a qualified specialist may at times be helpful. It is always good to avoid extremes, since such behavior is inconsistent with a natural and spontaneous life style.

One theme usually overemphasized in industrial societies is that of protein consumption. Many people overload the body with protein foods, not realizing that when they are healthy they will naturally be inclined to desire the nutrients they require, as they need them. Since amino acids are separated and then recombined in the body, all necessary amino acids can be assimilated from vegetable origins quite easily. Meats and other animal products are not needed for a balanced diet, although many prefer to eliminate meat, while still using milk, butter and eggs in limited amounts. Proteins are not stored by the body so excess becomes waste, which works a hardship on the body when processed and can even lead to toxicity.

A common mistake made by persons new to a vegetarian food plan is to attempt to replace meat by eating too many dairy products, especially cheese and eggs, or to consume too many nuts or other vegetable protein sources.

Herbs can be used for seasoning foods and for their thera-peutic effects, but salt and refined sugars should be eliminated entirely from the kitchen and the dining area.

When we eat foods we are interacting with the cosmos. We interact with the cosmos through all of our senses, but it is with the food that we take into the body, in material form, that forces enter which are directly influential. The atomic structures of carbohydrates, proteins, vitamins and minerals are, when closely examined, not very different, varying only in combination, but not in their essence. Below the level of the atom are finer forces which have their origins in the field of pure consciousness. Nature has provided itself with every-thing necessary for function and completion of purposes, and an all-pervading intelligence directs every process of nature. When, through intelligent behavior, we learn to cooperate with nature's laws we are able to consciously enter into a useful working relationship with the cosmos. The selection and eating of food, then, while requiring only a small portion of our time and attention, is a conscious practice which can be useful to our ultimate ends.

Charting Properties
and Actions of Foods

Foods are classified according to their tastes when first eaten, their sensations or actions (hot or cold), and the post-digestive action, the effects of foods after digestion. Some tastes change as a result of being digested. This will be noted as we follow along with a description of some common foods. We will begin with fruits, followed by vegetables, grains and other foods. The post-digestive taste will be listed only if it changes due to the changes occurring during digestion.

Apple: Sweet and astringent, cooling, sweet (post-diges-tive effect). Light, rough. Increases Air, decreases Fire. All right for Water constitutional types in moderate quantities.

Banana: Sweet and astringent, cooling, sour post-digestive taste. Smooth, heavy, laxative in quantity. Increases Water and Fire. Decreases Air.

Coconut: Sweet, cooling. Oily, smooth. Increases Water governing principle and decreases Air and Fire.

Figs: Sweet, cooling. Heavy, nourishing. Increases Water. Decreases Fire and Air.

Grapes (purple): Sweet, sour and astringent. Cooling. Sweet post-digestive effect. Smooth, watery. Increases Water. Decreases Fire and Air.

Melons: Sweet, cooling. Heavy, watery. Reduces Fire and Air.

Oranges: Sweet and sour. Heavy, promotes appetite. Increases Water and Fire. Decreases Air.

Peaches: Sweet and astringent, heating, sweet post-digestive effect. Heavy, watery. Increases Water and Fire. Decreases Air.

Pears: Sweet and astringent, cooling, sweet postdigestive effect. Heavy, dry, rough. Increases Air, decreases Water and Fire.

Plums: Sweet and astringent, heating, sweet postdigestive effect. Heavy, watery. Increases Fire and Water. Decreases Air.

Pomegranate: Sweet, sour and astringent, cooling, sweet post-digestive effect. Smooth, oily. Increases Air, decreases Fire and Water.

Beet: Sweet, heating. Heavy, smooth. Can increase Water and Fire if eaten in excess. Decreases Air.

Broccoli: Sweet and astringent, cooling, pungent postdigestive effect. Rough, dry. Increases Air, decreases Fire and Water.

Cabbage: Sweet and astringent, cooling, pungent postdigestive effect. Rough, dry. Increases Air, decreases Fire and Water.

Carrot: Sweet, bitter and astringent, cooling, pungent post-digestive effect. Heavy. Increases Fire if consumed in excess. Decreases Water and Air.

Cauliflower: Astringent, cooling, pungent postdigestive effect. Rough, dry. Increases Air. Decreases Fire and Water.

Celery: Astringent, cooling, pungent post-digestive effect. Rough, dry, light. Increases Air. Decreases Fire and Water.

Lettuce: Sweet and astringent, cooling, sweet post-digestive effect. Heavy. Increases Water, decreases Air and Fire.

Okra: Sweet and astringent, cooling, pungent post-digestive effect. Rough, dry, slippery. All right for all three constitutional types.

Raw Onion: Pungent, heating. Heavy, stimulating. Strengthening. Increases Air and Fire, decreases Water.

Potato: Sweet, salty and astringent, cooling. Sweet post-digestive effect. Rough, dry, light. Increases Air. Decreases Fire and Water.

Spinach: Astringent, cooling, pungent post-digestive effect. Rough, dry. Increases Air and Fire, decreases Water.

Sprouts: Mildly astringent, cooling, sweet post-digestive effect. Light. All right for all constitutional types but may aggravate Air if consumed in excess.

Tomato: Sweet and sour, heating, sour post-digestive effect. Light, moist. Increases all three governing principles.

Zucchini: Sweet and astringent, cooling, pungent post-digestive effect. Wet, light. Decreases Fire. *May* increase Water. All right for Air types.

Barley: Sweet and astringent, cooling, sweet post-digestive effect. Light. Increases Air. Decreases Fire and Water.

Basmati Rice: Sweet, cooling. Light, soft, smooth and nourishing. Decreases Air and Fire. All right for Water types in moderation.

Brown Rice: Sweet, heating. Heavy. Increases Fire and Water. Decreases Air.

Buckwheat: Sweet and astringent, heating, sweet post-digestive effect. Light, dry. Increases Air and Fire. Decreases Water governing principle.

Corn: Sweet, heating. Light, dry. Increases Air and Fire. Decreases Water.

Oats: Sweet, heating. Heavy. Dry oats increase Air and Fire, and decrease Water. Cooked oats increase Water and decrease Air and Fire.

Millet: Sweet, heating. Light, dry. Increases Air and Fire. Decreases Water governing principle.

Rye: Sweet and astringent, heating, sweet post-digestive effect. Light, dry. Increases Air and Fire. Decreases Water governing principle.

Wheat: Sweet, cooling. Heavy. Increases Water. Reduces Air and Fire.

Almonds: Sweet, heating. Heavy, oily. Increases Fire and Water. Decreases Air. Energizer, rejuvenator.

Cashews: Sweet, heating. Heavy, oily. Increases Fire and Water. Decreases Air. Energizing.

Peanuts: Sweet and astringent, heating, sweet post-digestive effect. Heavy, oily. Increases Fire and Water. All right for Air types if used in moderation.

Pumpkin Seed: Sweet, bitter and astringent, heating. Pungent post-digestive effect. Heavy, dry. Increases Fire and Water. Decreases Air.

Sunflower Seed: Sweet and astringent, heating, sweet post-digestive effect. Heavy, oily. Mildly increases Fire and Water. Decreases Air.

Lentils: Sweet and astringent, heating, sweet post-digestive effect. Dry, rough, heavy and should only be taken in small quantities because of tendency to dehydrate the body. Increases Air and Water. Decreases Fire.

Mung Beans: Sweet and astringent, cooling, sweet post-digestive effect. Light, soft. Increases Water. Decreases Fire and Air.

Soy Beans: Sweet and astringent, cooling, sweet post-digestive effect. Heavy, oily, smooth. Increases Air and Water. Decreases Fire. Tofu is all right in moderation.

Kidney Beans: Sweet and astringent, sweet post-digestive effect. Dry and rough. Laxative effect. Increases Air and Water. Decreases Fire.

Honey: Sweet and astringent, heating, sweet post-digestive effect. Dry, rough, heavy. Breaks up mucus. Mildly increases Fire. Decreases Water and Air governing principles.

Sesame Oil: Sweet, bitter and astringent, heating, sweet post-digestive effect. Heavy, oily, smooth. Increases Fire. Decreases Air. All right for Water types in moderation.

Sunflower Oil: Sweet, cooling. Light, oily, strengthening to the system. All right for all three constitutional types.

Safflower Oil: Sweet and pungent, heating, pungent post-digestive effect. Relatively light, sharp, oily, irritating if used in excess. Increases Fire. Decreases Water and Air.

Corn Oil: Sweet, heating. Relatively light, oily, smooth. Increases Fire. All right for Water and Air types in moderation.

Ghee (clarified butter):   Sweet, cooling. Light, oily, and smooth. Useful for all three governing principle types if taken in moderation. Taken in excess it increases Water influence. Promotes digestion, strengthens the system and is useful when taking herbal remedies.

Goat's Milk: Sweet and astringent, cooling, sweet post-digestive effect. Light. Increases Air. Decreases Fire and Water governing principles.

Cow's Milk: Sweet, cooling. Light, oily, smooth. Increases Water. Decreases Fire and Air.

This is but a brief overview of foods, their qualities and effects according to Ayurveda, but it will provide an idea of the approach taken when planning food needs, either for maintaining the balance of the governing principles or for therapeutic purposes.

FIVE

Food Preparation and Helpful Routines

The most practical way to select foods is to follow your natural instinct and eat what your body "tells you" it wants. When the body is cleansed of toxic wastes, when one's life style is ordered, when inner peace is present, we naturally feel inclined to select foods which are most useful for physical and emotional wellness, and there will be no psychological cravings present—intelligence will be the determining factor.

It should be borne in mind that the Ayurvedic approach to food selection is based on the taste influences on the governing principles of the body. This does not mean that foods to be avoided in special instances are not nutritious, but merely that they may tend to contribute to an increase of governing principles which you may not want to be predominant in your life. A general guideline is to provide all six tastes in each meal, with a predominance of tastes which have been chosen for special needs. During a family meal, or any group meal, it is usually possible to select from available foods those which suit one's needs. Even in restaurants, where a variety of foods is available, one should have no problem eating according to one's individual needs. When one is following a food regimen for special purposes, the variety of foods available for the menu is sufficient to ensure a balanced selection to meet nutritional needs, and in most instances vitamin and mineral supplementation will not be necessary.

Foods should be selected for freshness and in their natural state. Processed foods should be avoided; this makes shopping in the supermarket simple, because it is very easy to tell the difference between fresh and processed foods, and even with packaged foods one can read the label to ensure that additives and preservatives are not included for whatever reason. Beware also of foods which have been treated to extend shelf life. Radiated foods are suspect, and liquids, such as milk and juices, should be in opaque glass containers, not in clear glass containers or in plastic. Light can destroy vitamins in liquids and plastic may infuse the contents with contaminants.

Kitchen utensils and food containers should be made of natural materials, not plastic or aluminum. Everything used in the preparation of food should be clean, including the counter tops, cutting boards, and cutting and mixing utensils. Vegetables and fruits should be washed, and unused grains and nuts kept in sealed containers. In our opinion, foods which are cooked should be cooked on a stove top or in its oven, not in a microwave oven. There is a possibility that the use of microwaves can alter the characteristics of foods. In fact, it is increasingly believed that many modern appliances, such as microwave ovens, smoke detectors, television sets and electronic machines of various kinds can interfere with body function because of excess radiation in the environment. Even the radiation from decomposing granite and other natural substances can leak into a building through the floors and foundation and cause a health hazard.

Many foods can be eaten in their raw state and be easily assimilated by the body. However, some foods are more useful to the body when cooked. When vegetables are cooked the heat causes the starch inside the cells to swell. This ruptures the cellulose wall of the plant cell and releases the nutrients so they can be digested. Some vitamins, such as Vitamin C, are lost in the cooking process, but many other vitamins are not influenced. The cell is destroyed by heat, exposing its contents to oxidation. For this reason, cooked foods should be eaten soon after they are prepared and not stored for a long time afterwards.

Another advantage of cooking some foods is that when they are cooked they become more concentrated—that is, a smaller amount of the cooked food contains the nutrients in condensed form that the larger volume contained before being reduced by cooking. One must usually consume a larger volume of foods if they are eaten raw because of their water content, hence larger volume. The ideal, in most instances, is not to overcook or use extreme high heat when preparing vegetables.

An Easy Cleansing Routine
to Use From Time to Time

There are occasions when we feel the need to cleanse the body but at the same time we are not inclined or it is not convenient to go on an extensive fast. Fasting is not usually recommended for some constitutional types. Air constitutional types should not fast very much because they will experience an increase of the Air governing principle and become "spaced out." Fire constitutional types can fast a few days, at most. This is because fasting often increases the Fire governing principle in the body, which will tend to aggravate it in a person who already has a strong Fire influence. Water constitutional types can usually fast more comfortably than other types. A fast of more than two or three days should be carefully supervised, under any circumstances.

An easy way to encourage the cleansing of toxic wastes from the body is simply to consume only cleansing foods. Fruits and vegetables fall into this category. Nuts, beans and dairy products do not.

To start, plan ahead to assist yourself to be psychologically prepared. This is not an extreme routine and will not interfere with your normal activities. In fact, most people find it quite pleasant. During this regimen be sure to ensure intestinal cleansing. An easy way to do this is to obtain a supply of powdered psyllium seed husks and use once or twice a day. A rounded teaspoon of the powder in a glass of water, stirred well and swallowed right away, is recommended. Psyllium is not a cathartic; the fiber attracts water to the intestinal tract, adding bulk, which assists in evacuation in a natural manner.

Also, bathe twice a day and obtain sufficient exercise. Hatha Yoga and extended walking are useful. The procedures will assist in releasing waste matter from the systems of the body. Meditate on a regular schedule and feel that the inner life force is becoming increasingly influential.

The morning meal can be fresh fruit. Fruits are cleansers, as well as supplying nutrients in easily assimilated form. Fruits are quickly digested and pass through the body easily.

The noon meal can be a fresh garden salad. For a dressing, lemon juice and olive oil can be used. If something more solid is desired, a small portion of cooked brown or basmati rice can be added to the meal. Chopped onion would be a good accompaniment to the rice.

The early evening meal could include another small fresh garden salad and a baked potato. To garnish the potato, sauted onion and garlic would be useful.

After several days the body will feel light and clean, the eyes and tongue will be clean, the stool will be odorless and will float in water. An increase in energy and mental alertness will be noted. Meditation will be easy and enjoyable.

Everything in nature is built up of atomic particles—we live in an electric universe. Electric vital force is present in natural foods and is released into the body when foods are consumed. The beneficial ingredients of natural foods are transformed solar light. Electricity stands for action, a breaking and making of equilibrium. Fruits attack and break up toxic conditions. Some vegetables, on the other hand, such as potatoes and onions, attract toxic matter by magnetic force and carry it away from the body. This is why, in this regimen, fruits are taken in the morning and vegetables later in the day.

After a sense of balance and well-being has been restored, one can then begin to include other preferred items in the diet, doing so gradually until the dietary program is once again established to suit one's preference and needs.

During the cleansing routine, and afterwards, distilled water is the preferred liquid to drink. Most city water, even though purified and pronounced suitable for drinking, contains residues which cannot possibly contribute to the health of the body. Even well water should be inspected, to ensure its purity and to be sure it does not contain high levels of metals, such as copper and iron. Distilled water should always be stored in glass, earthenware or stainless steel containers, never in plastic. Distilled water attracts waste matter, especially urea, and carries it out through the kidneys. Water is best taken at room temperature, rather than hot or cold, except for special purposes.

Besides the influences of the governing principles of foods, also considered in this approach is whether foods and liquids are hot, cold, light, heavy, oily, or dry. Hot foods increase the Fire influence. Cold foods reduce Fire influence and increase Water influence. Light, dry foods increase Air influence and decrease Water influence. Heavy, oily foods increase the Water influence and decrease Air influence.

A person with a strong Fire constitution, for example, would be likely to aggravate his constitution by consuming too much hot and spicy food. Too much cold food and cold liquids would not be useful to a Water type constitution, nor would too much heavy and oily food. Too much light, dry food would not be useful to an Air constitution. We can understand, then, how indiscriminate choice of foods and liquids might be upsetting to one's body systems because of disturbing the balance of the governing principles.

Warm cooked foods are suitable; other foods and liquids are best taken at near room temperature. Excess of any food or liquid is not recommended. Even herbal teas should not be used in excess because they are "medicines," with their ingredients concentrated in the water.

The Practical Benefits of Moderation in Diet

Eating foods in proper quantities and combinations ensures adequate nutrition, ideal body weight, an abundance of energy and, quite possibly, a longer life. Live foods, plus the prana taken in through breathing and meditation, provide nutrients and life force, and maintain a balance of the governing principles. Body weight stabilizes because persons who are underweight gain, and persons who are overweight lose the excess. By not overeating the body conserves energy which would otherwise be utilized in processing unnecessary foods.

There is evidence to indicate that planned undereating, that is, eating less than "normal" people eat, is helpful in many ways. The ideal of eating slowly, chewing well, and stopping before feeling full, is a good way to monitor the appetite. We are not here suggesting that we deny the body what it requires, only that we avoid eating what is not required. Naturally thin people often metabolize foods more quickly and have a higher body temperature, both of which may reduce life span. Persons who overeat, but whose metabolism is slower, may also have a reduced life span because of complications caused by overeating. The purpose of undereating is not to become thin, but to provide only what the body requires, and no excess. Unrestricted food intake may be linked to a variety of ailments, such as kidney disease, heart disease, cataracts and cancer. The plan should be, then, to eat when hungry and then only what is necessary. Occasional cleansing routines can also be useful, to remove toxic wastes.

Many of the rejuvenation routines recommended in Ayurveda contribute to an increase of "gastric fire," the ability of the body to process foods. After all, even an abundant supply of nutritious foods, if they are not adequately utilized by the body, are of little value in the long run.

Special Food Influences
to Know About and Consider

Some foods act as cleansers, some as builders, and some as vitalizers. One should use them as the inclination arises and carefully note the effects. Fruits, as mentioned above, are cleansers. Vegetables that grow above the ground are cleansing and sustaining foods. They have strong solar influence, but not as much as fruits which grow higher above the ground. Underground vegetables have more earth influence and are also sustaining foods. Potatoes, carrots, beets, turnips and other root vegetables fall into this category. Onions, garlic and ginger are vitalizing foods, especially for men. They are also powerful cleansers and help in the removal of toxins and harmful bacteria from the body.

Nuts can be useful to the diet but should not be used to excess since they are concentrated. A dozen almonds, for instance, is a sufficient quantity at one time, well chewed or blended with liquid. Some nuts are difficult to digest, such as the peanut, which is best used as a butter and then not in large quantity. Soybean, while a legume and not a nut, is often difficult to digest. Undigested proteins, since they cannot be stored by the body, result in toxic residue which has to be flushed from the system.

In Ayurvedic texts the following drink is recommended for men, to help maintain health of the reproductive system. Soak six to ten almonds overnight in milk. Remove the skins. Put in a blender with a teaspoon of honey and the crushed seeds of three or four cardamom pods, and blend until frothy. Drink at room temperature and do not eat anything for two or three hours afterwards. Also recommended are pistachio nuts. Garlic, onions and ginger are also useful to naturally energize the systems of the body.

If dairy products are used, the source should be known to assure wholesome milk and eggs. These, too, are animal proteins and many who are on a vegetarian food plan prefer not to use them. Cheese, if used, should be one of the soft cheeses, such as cottage cheese or some variation of it. Hard cheeses are difficult to digest.

It will be noted that tomatoes are not included as a recommended food item in any of the three listings for constitutional types. Tomatoes have nutritive value, of course, but they tend to increase all three governing principles and, therefore, are recommended only in modest quantities, if at all. In fact, if one is healthy and his governing principles are balanced, he can eat any nutritious foods with no problem, being careful not to eat in excess.

The foods listed for each constitutional type are the ones

which will not increase one's dominant governing principles, while allowing the ones less influential to increase, thus contributing to harmony among them. When planning menus it can be useful to experiment by partaking of the food groups recommended for your constitutional type, to see if changes in the general feeling of well-being can be noted.

If one has a mixed constitutional type, for instance if one's basic type is Water-Fire, with Water predominant, and only a small amount of Air influence present, one could select foods according to the percentages as determined from the self-examination test in chapter two of this section. For instance, if one's basic constitutional type is fifty per cent Water, thirty per cent Fire, and twenty per cent Air, foods could be selected from the Water, Fire and Air listings accordingly.

Vegetables, grains and legumes should constitute the basic dietary plan. When grains, such as rice or corn, are eaten at the same meal as beans or lentils, the combination enables the combined amino acids from these combinations to provide a balance of protein requirements. Fruits should be the smaller portion of the overall dietary routine, and should be eaten at a time other than at the main meal, for easier digestibility. Melons should not be combined with other fruits, although occasional lapses will not represent a major problem.

Fruit and vegetable juices should be used only in moderation, as they comprise the concentrated essence of a much larger volume of the vegetables or fruits one would ordinarily eat at one time. Fruit juices can be diluted fifty per cent with water to represent less of a challenge to the digestive process. Apple juice is good for Water constitutional types because it decreases Water and Fire and increases Air. Grape juice is good for Fire and Air types because it decreases these governing principles and increases Water influence. The guide is to partake of juices as with foods, so use the fruits and their juices according to the chart which best agrees with your basic type. The milder fruits are better when their juice is to be used.

When using recipes simply substitute foods which are desired for personal use, when possible. An innovative food preparer will have no problem in planning attractive menus which will be pleasing in every way, as well as satisfying requirements for maintaining the balance of governing principles which influence body functions.

To make ghee (clarified butter), simply put a pound of unsalted butter in a heavy pan and simmer for about twenty minutes, watching to be sure it does not burn. A froth will come to the top and the solids will sink to the bottom, leaving the golden butterfat clear. Remove from the stove and let set for ten minutes or so, then strain in a clean glass jar, using a wet double-thickness cheesecloth to catch the solids. This will remain usable for a long time if stored in the refrigerator and can be used as a cooking oil to saute vegetables.

Some persons, especially Water constitutional types, enjoy fasting one day a week, either using distilled water or thin juices. This affords the body rest and has an energizing effect upon body and mind. The usual pattern is to select a non-working day for this purpose in order to give more time to meditation and reflection.

In all instances, remember that food is just one way to contribute to the balance of internal processes. Of major importance are attention to spiritual practices and to maintaining a cheerful outlook and balanced mental attitude at all times.

SUGGESTED FOODS
FOR WATER (Kapha) CONSTITUTIONAL TYPES

Recommended is to avoid breakfast until at least 10 A.M. Also, to avoid sugar, fats, dairy products and salt, and to add lighter, drier foods. Lunch should be the major meal of the day, with only a light, dry meal in the evening. Also to be avoided are cold drinks, large quantities of food and indulgence in sweet, sour and salty tastes. Occasional short fasts can be handled.

Vegetables	Fruits	Grains
pungent & bitter	apples	barley
vegetables	apricots	corn
asparagus	berries	millet
beets	cherries	oats, dry
broccoli	cranberries	rye
brussels sprouts	figs	basmati rice in
cabbage	mangos	small quantities
carrots	peaches	
cauliflower	pears	
celery	persimmon	All legumes except
eggplant	pomegranate	kidney beans, mung
garlic	prunes	beans, soybeans and
leafy greens	raisins	black lentils.
onions		Clarified butter and
parsley		goat's milk all right.
peas		Almond, corn and
peppers		sunflower oils in
potatoes		small quantities.
spinach		

The Water governing principle is aggravated in the spring of the year. At this time eat less and add more dry, fibrous foods.

SUGGESTED FOODS
FOR FIRE (Pitta) CONSTITUTIONAL TYPES

Breakfast is usually all right for this constitutional type. Should avoid egg yolks, nuts, chilies, hot spices, honey and hot drinks. Cool foods and liquids are better, and add sweet, bitter and astringent tastes. Should avoid sour-tasting foods. Among spices, black pepper, coriander, and cardamom are all right.

Vegetables	Fruits	Grains
sweet & bitter vegetables O.K.	sweet fruits	barley
asparagus	apples	oats, cooked
broccoli	avocado	basmati rice
brussels sprouts	figs	wheat
cabbage	dark grapes	
cucumber	mangos	
cauliflower	melons	All legumes except lentils are all right.
celery	oranges	Coconut, sunflower and pumpkin seeds are all right.
green beans	pineapple	
leafy greens	plums	
mushrooms	pomegranate	Dairy products in moderation.
okra	prunes	
peas	raisins	Coconut, olive, soy and sunflower oils.
parsley		
green peppers		
potatoes		
sprouts		
zucchini squash		

The Fire governing principle is aggravated during summer. Stay calm and cool, increasing cooling foods and drinks.

SUGGESTED FOODS
FOR AIR (Vata) CONSTITUTIONAL TYPES

Breakfast is usually all right and, sometimes, light meals during the day. Avoid dry and bitter foods. Sweet and hot foods are useful. Dairy products, in moderation, can usually be tolerated. These types should add more sweet and oily foods, as well as salty and sour tastes. Warm or hot water is all right. Nuts and nut butters are usually all right. Spices such as cinnamon, cardamom, cumin, ginger, cloves and mustard can be used with benefit.

Vegetables	*Fruits*	*Grains*
cooked vegetables	sweet fruits	oats, cooked
asparagus	apricot	rice
beets	avocado	wheat
carrots	bananas	
cucumber	berries	
garlic	cherries	
green beans	coconut	No legumes except
onion, cooked	fresh figs	mung beans, black
sweet potato	grapefruit	and red lentils, and
radishes	lemons	tofu.
leafy greens	grapes	All oils are all right.
in moderation	mangos	
	sweet melons	
	sour oranges	
	papaya	
	peaches	
	sour pineapple	
	sour plums	
	persimmons	

The Air governing principle is aggravated during autumn and winter. Increase warm and oily foods during this season.

SIX

The Secrets of
the Mortal-Immortals

Since the physical body is primarily enlivened by soul force, the same force that nourishes the universe, it should be no cause for surprise to learn that methods are available which are claimed to rejuvenate the body.

The major reasons for decay of the body are: lack of spiritual awareness, psychological causes, stress, toxicity, genetic influences, and personal karmic conditions. All of these contributing factors can be confronted and handled. Ayurvedic procedures have long been researched, and applied with varying degrees of success, to promote rejuvenation and life extension.

In this approach, emphasis is placed upon the importance of spiritual awareness, because of the understanding that psychological conditions and physical (as well as life style) conditions are reflections of states of consciousness. Therefore, no approach to rejuvenation would be complete if the importance of God-realization were omitted. It is possible, when working with a person who is not spiritually inclined, to restore him to a fair degree of health and wellness, but the deeper and more subtle causes of possible future problems would not be addressed. In Ayurveda the emphasis is upon health and long life for the purpose of fulfilling soul destiny, not merely to assist persons to continue in a pattern of routine and perhaps self-defeating practices.

Secrets of the
Mortal-Immortals

For centuries, in different cultures in various parts of the
world, legends of extraordinary people who have transcended
normal boundaries of human experience have flourished. From
India and China, especially, have come stories of mortal-immortals, individuals who have "conquered death." In Paramahansa Yogananda's book, *Autobiography of a Yogi*, the existence of a great seer, Mahavatar Babaji, was revealed to the
Western world for the first time:

"The northern Himalayan crags near Badrinarayan are
still blessed by the living presence of Babaji, guru of Lahiri
Mahasaya," Paramahansaji wrote. "The secluded master has
retained his physical form for centuries, perhaps for millen-
niums. The deathless guru bears no marks of age on his body;
he appears to be a youth of no more than twenty-five. Fair-
skinned, of medium build and height, Babaji's beautiful strong
body radiates a perceptible glow. His undecayable body requires no food."

It is known that this illumined master has several times
undergone a radical rejuvenation process, known as *kaya
kalpa*, which enables the body to "span the ages." In a published account by Paramahansa Pranavananda, a disciple of
Lahiri Mahasaya, the following information is shared:

Pranavananda was once visiting his guru when he was sur-
prised to see Lahiri go up to the courtyard and bow before a
youthful sage. Lahiri asked Pranavananda to also acknowledge
the young visitor, whom he introduced as Mahavatar Babaji.
Even though Babaji appeared much younger than Lahiri, the
latter frequently referred to him as "the old father," ancient
spiritual father. Babaji, although he does not usually eat food,
shared a modest meal with the two men. During the conversation, Pranavananda asked Babaji how old he was. Babaji
replied that one hundred and twenty years was the normal
span of life but that one could experience life extension by
undergoing the kaya kalpa regimen. He further mentioned
that he had done so three times and was presently undergoing

Represented on the altar are Mahavatar Babaji, Lahiri Mahasaya, Jesus, Sri Yukteswar and Paramahansa Yogananda. CSA Meditation Hall, Lakemont, Georgia, 1987.

the fourth such program. This incident occurred in the latter part of the nineteenth century, and Babaji is still active with the spiritual affairs of Planet Earth today. He, and others like him, are not limited to any sectarian concerns, but devote their efforts to the process of cleansing planetary conscious-ness in harmony with the current ascending cycle processes which are now influential.

Rejuvenation methods and techniques are practiced by many yogis and seers in order to extend the life cycle so that they can accomplish special purposes with which they have been entrusted by providence—the guardianship of God over his creation. Such methods are also available to people today, to those fortunate enough to learn of them and to recognize their possibilities. Life extension has little value unless one is involved with spiritual practices for the purpose of awakening the soul nature, and is practicing the cultivation of the virtues. The ideal life is not an unhappy life, but a life which is pur-poseful. Freedom from discomfort and disease enables one to pursue worthy goals with all vital forces active.

Toward the end of the third decade of this century, the secular press in India, Europe and America carried news of an Indian holy man who had thrice undergone the *kaya kalpa* process. The first time he did so he was over eighty years of age, feeble and worn out because of his arduous disciplines and long pilgrimages. He met a person knowledgeable in the use of these purification procedures and submitted to the process. After several weeks he emerged from a sheltered hut, which was used as his abode for the duration of the experience, appearing at least thirty years younger, restored to full vigor, with new dark hair and a third set of teeth, which had grown in during his seclusion. This holy man experienced the process twice more and lived another hundred years before consciously leaving the body during meditation.

During the period of seclusion, most of which was spent in deep meditation, he often communed with saints, who would visit him in their subtle form. After emerging from his seclusion he admitted that, while body cleansing and the use of certain herbal substances had been helpful, the most important part of the process was repeated and prolonged *samadhi* experience.

There are some enlightenment masters who know their destiny and who are so open to the field of pure consciousness that they can merely *will* to remain healthy and can decide how many years they will maintain the body. Such masters know themselves to be expressions of Spirit and that they are but using the body for intended purposes. They are not confined to the body, nor limited to it or the mind in any way. They, and others like them, can dematerialize the body if they so desire, and then rematerialize it at will. They can also move through inner space and travel to any place on this planet, or other planets, even to other solar systems if they so desire. Whatever they are led to do to fulfill their purposes they can do, without effort. In rare instances, when the present body is no longer suitable for continued use, they can leave it and enter the body of a younger person who, for karmic reasons, has left it. This can be done if the master's consciousness assumes the younger body immediately after the previous occupant has left it, and before any injury to the nervous system and body tissues has occurred due to lack of available soul force to enliven them. A Self-realized master can also immediately reincarnate after having left the body, for the purpose of continuing his or her mission. In the latter instance, in the new incarnation the person shines as a spiritual prodigy at an early age.

Because an extremely long-lived person has a mission which extends over centuries, and has no karmic ties with the world, it is common for such a person to relocate after a few years or decades, even assuming a new name, in order to work without public notice in ways which seem most useful.

A Sanskrit scripture explains, as follows:

Adeptship is achieved by purification of man's bodies. It is also attainable through the grace of the guru.

Purification comes through Nature, penance, and mantras.

Through Nature there is purification of dense matter

(the physical body); through penance, purification of
the fine matter (the subtle body); through mantras,
purification of the mind.

Because discomfort and disease interfere with our ability
to fulfill purposes, all who are desirous of enhancing their
abilities should be concerned with ensuring the removal, on
all levels, of restrictions and latent causes of possible future
problems. An adept is a *siddha*, one who has experienced
perfection as a result of spiritual practices. The grace of the
guru is mentioned because an enlightened guru can guide the
disciple so that quick progress is experienced. Also, the infusion of the guru's consciousness and vital force helps to cleanse
the disciple's inner nature. By reverent association with a true
guru, one who is established in pure consciousness, the disciple
receives the benefits of that pure consciousness as it acts on
subtle levels of mind and body. This infusion of *shakti*, creative
force, from the guru contributes greatly to transformation
and soul awakening.

The following common causes of decay and aging of the
body can be removed by giving responsible attention to certain processes:

Lack of Spiritual Awareness — Yearning to know the truth
about life is the most powerful influence in stirring soul force
so that awakening is experienced. Also, one should pray and
meditate, and do everything possible to live a life modeled
after the advice of the scriptures. One does not "become spiritual" as a result of observing scriptural guidelines, but such
procedures will contribute to a more orderly life style and
assist in psychological transformation. In this way a "good"
life can precede the true spiritual life.

Psychological Causes — Mental and emotional conflicts
inhibit the flow and circulation of superconscious forces in
the mind and body. While it is true that regular meditation
will, in time, result in cleansing of the mental field and the
feeling nature, it is well for one intent on the path to engage
in sincere self-analysis and make attempts to modify mental

attitudes, thought processes, and behavior in order to remove serious conflicts. When ignorance alone is not the major factor, relative to psychological problems, the chief contributing problem is egocentricity. Many attitudes and beliefs may have to be renounced if one is to experience peace of mind and psychological wellness. The practice of patience, being inwardly calm regardless of what transpires, is important to the process of cleansing the subtle body, the seat of feeling. This is why even-mindedness is so highly extolled. An even-minded person is not disinterested in his surroundings, but remains centered and observant regardless of what transpires. He accepts failure as calmly as he accepts success, and does not become emotionally upset when criticised or misunderstood. No external circumstance causes him to waver internally, because he is established in understanding.

The mental field is purified as the result of superior superconscious forces flowing through it on all levels. Tamas guna is cleansed from the mind, rajas guna is purified, and sattva guna prevails until it, too, is transcended and only the influence of pure consciousness remains.

During deep meditation, before transcendence is experienced, the meditator feels himself to be immersed in Om, the primal current of the universe. This pure mantra redeems the mind by cleansing it of all dross.

Accumulated Stress — When the nervous system becomes overstressed as a result of inharmonious living, mental processes become disorganized, emotions become confused, and body systems begin to malfunction. The result is the manifestation of subtle problems, imbalance of the governing principles which regulate internal processes, and a corresponding disorganization of the supporting tissues of the body. All therapeutic regimens recommended in a holistic approach to life enhancement are useful in eradicating stress symptoms. The most useful technique of all is regular superconscious meditation.

The Presence of Toxic Wastes — To remove toxic wastes, all of the therapeutic procedures available can be useful, applied according to individual need, based on psychological temperament and physical constitution.

Genetic Influences — Even inherited genetic predispositions can be addressed and neutralized through skillful means. For many, the ability to *believe* this to be possible will be a major part of the therapy process. It should be remembered that the body is constantly undergoing change. It is constantly being renewed and, therefore, even genetic influences can be altered and prevented from bearing fruit. Concerning life extension, one may need to actively work to change his thinking about the matter. Many people live but "three score and ten" years, merely because they believe this to be the norm for human beings. Others live longer because they expect to do so, and because they have reasons for doing so.

Personal Karmic Conditions — One's karmic condition is the sum total of all that has been accumulated in the way of desires, traumas, mental conditionings, emotional states, beliefs, opinions and dominant states of consciousness. These imprint the mind, emotional body, and physical body and become "possible causes" of near and distant future effects. These, too, can be resisted, contained, and dissolved in a variety of ways.

In short, one who desires to experience complete rejuvenation of the body, and even life extension, must accept the premise that Spirit is superior to all expressions of matter, even to mind, which is equally a material manifestation.

**Esoteric Keys
to the Process**

Inner understanding provides us with data about rejuvenation and life extension procedures. To attempt to understand the procedures from objective analysis alone results only in superficial discoveries. It is important to take into consideration the fact that the universe is one organic whole, that our bodies are a part of the universe. In fact, the universe is our larger body, and the body through which we function is a unit in the cosmic process. The forces that flow through the universe flow through us. From a relative point of view we

can say that our body and the universe are interdependent.
From a cosmic viewpoint we can understand that there is
only one body, the universe, and that all forms are expressions
within it.

When thinking of rejuvenation, therefore, we are to think
in terms of arranging conditions so that the all-enlivening vital
force of the universe can flow through body and mind, cleansing and renewing at all levels. Over the centuries, many people
have prescribed various dietary and other therapeutic regimens for the purpose of maintaining health and function, but
these have been, at best, short-term expedients, successful to
some degree but failing to result in complete and lasting benefits. Unless the enlivening influences of nature, the creative
forces from the source, are understood and cooperated with,
there will always be a limit to therapies which are designed
to work from the outside in, instead of from the inside out.

Enlightened practitioners of life extension procedures
know what most people do not know, that they are in reality
rays of pure consciousness expressing through mind and body.
A person who is fully Self-realized will naturally and spontaneously live his life in accord with the laws of nature and
its rhythms. He will automatically do those things which contribute to wellness and avoid activities which might cause him
to transgress the laws of nature. Such a person does not behave in a superstitious fashion, but simply lives as man is
meant to live, in a world which is, for him, a paradise. For
the enlightened person, heaven in all its fullness is present at
every moment.

A little known saint who lived for one hundred and thirty-
seven years and who made his conscious transition in Nepal
in 1963, was the gentle man known as the Shivapuri Baba
("the holy father who lives in the Shivapuri forest"). During
the first third of his life, over twenty-five years were spent
living in the jungles of India, practicing meditation and contemplating the scriptures. The saint later went on a world
pilgrimage, walking sixty per cent of the way, across Europe,
the Americas and China, before returning to India and Nepal.
He then settled in a quiet forest environment and there spent

the remainder of his years, welcoming sincere truth seekers from time to time.

Versed in the scriptures and established in God-realization, the Shivapuri Baba taught a simple way of life, one based on attention to spiritual, moral and bodily disciplines. In essence, he taught that one should continue unfailingly with spiritual practices until full realization is experienced, cultivate the moral virtues, and attend to practical measures to ensure bodily health. All this, while serving the world in some useful way. Once, when commenting on his own long life, he mentioned that it was possible, by living a natural life and through the use of certain pranayamas, to live for at least one thousand years. He mentioned this as a real possibility, not as comment to be taken as idle speculation.

Legends, supported by personal accounts, tell of a group of ascetics living in the Himalayas who have retained their bodies for thousands of years. Mahavatar Babaji is one of this group, among whom are some who have been on the planet since before the great Mahabharata wars in India. This would make these persons over four thousand years old, so far as the number of years they have been in the present bodily form. Some of them are knowledgeable in the use of certain herbal ingredients, kaya kalpa procedures and other processes. The major "medicine," however, is the creative current which enlivens them because all inner restrictions have been removed.

Also presently residing at various locations in the planet's magnetic field are illumined seers who have withdrawn from physical encasement and who still serve the purpose of contributing to the spiritual welfare of the human race. Not bound by karma or by any personal compulsion, they serve as conduits through which transforming influences flow to assist in planetary transformation. The existence of such illumined beings is acknowledged by many enlightenment traditions, and it is clearly stated that their existence is factual, that they are not mere "projections" due to wishful thinking on the part of spiritually immature zealots. The only way to communicate with these masters of wisdom and "upholders of the laws of life" is by self-preparation through discipline and spiritual practices.

It is by understanding the fine and subtle causes which regulate outer effects that one is able to live outside of the rules of cause and effect which apply to those of restricted knowing and thinking.

Preparation
and Purification

Before undergoing a radical program designed to result in rejuvenation, one should first become familiar with the underlying principles upon which the procedure is based. One should also have the benefit of the help of a qualified practitioner in attendance. The practitioner-helper should be well versed in the procedures, be an example of moral and spiritual virtues, and be able to correctly diagnose the condition and the needs of the patient-client. A thorough examination should be given, so that a full understanding of the subject's basic constitutional type is known, and any special needs should be observed and taken into account.

Therapeutic procedures should be prescribed and administered according to individual need. A superficial approach, while perhaps proving somewhat productive, will not accomplish the desired results. Because of the different basic governing constitutional types, individual needs will obviously vary greatly, and the approach taken will necessarily depend on such individual requirements. The purpose of the rejuvenation program is to encourage the balancing of the governing principle influences; for this, specific processes must be prescribed. A person who is predominantly a Water-Fire constitutional type, for instance, would not respond well to a program designed for one whose basic constitutional type is different. So long as procedures are correct there will be no harmful side effects—there will only be excellent results or less than excellent results, depending upon how well the appropriate procedures are chosen and used.

The Sanskrit word for the procedures used for rejuvenation therapy is *rasayana* (rah-sigh'-yah-na). *Rasa* means taste,

elixir or essence; *ayana* means "to circulate through pathways, to the home or abode." It is a means of restoring the
immune system so that body fluids circulate and find their
right place in perfect harmony. Such a procedure not only
restores the immune system to full strength, it also removes
all toxic wastes from the body, cleanses the mental field and
refines the brain structure and nerves of the body. The
body's ability to assimilate food is improved so that when
food is ingested, it is properly utilized and transformed in
successive stages to provide healthy tissues.

From an Ayurvedic text we quote:

> Rasayana is possessed of inconceivable and wonderful
> possibilities, being promotive of longevity and health,
> preservative of youth, dispersive of somnolence, tor-
> por, fatigue, exhaustion, indolence and weakness, re-
> storative of the balance of Air, Fire and Water (gov-
> erning principles), curative of flabbiness, stimulative
> of the internal gastric fire and promotive of luster,
> complexion and voice.

One reason for the observance of *brahmacharya* (right use
of senses and life force) is so that vital forces which are not
wasted can be transmuted into finer essence to nourish deeper
levels of the body.

The usual rejuvenation treatment lasts twenty-eight days,
timed in harmony with the lunar cycle. A general program
can be entered into which is moderate in application and will
not interfere unduly with a person's normal schedule. A more
specific program would require the subject to remain in seclusion for the duration of the program. The secluded environment should ideally be located where the climate is moderate
and where one can be isolated from social involvements. The
abode should be of even temperature, quiet, and with the
necessary conveniences. There should be no possibility of intrusion of any kind during the program, and no communication of any kind with the outside world, except for the needed

visits of the practitioner-helper. This is a time of complete retreat and total rest.

The dwelling used should have an inner room, for privacy, an outer room for convenience and comfort, and a courtyard or covered porch to allow contact with nature but not over-involvement.

Before the program is to begin one may undergo various necessary purification procedures, depending upon individual need. These may include a cleansing diet before the onset of the program, then more specific purification procedures, such as: vomiting, purging of the intestinal tract, both small and large; medicated or nutrient cleansing of the colon; lubricated cleansing of the colon; and nasal and ear cleansing to remove accumulations in the head and throat. The theory is that if the body is cleansed as completely as possible of toxic matter, nutrients will be better absorbed into the system when they are administered.

The Procedure
and How It Works

The purpose of rejuvenation therapy is to cleanse the body and allow nourishment to be properly utilized. The psychological nature and behavior of the person undergoing the process is likewise important. In the *Charaka Samhita* we read:

> One who speaks the truth, one who is free from anger, who abstains from alcohol and sexual congress (during the process), hurts no one, avoids overstrain, is tranquil of heart, fair-spoken, is devoted to holy chants and to cleanliness, is endowed with understanding, given to alms-giving, diligent in spiritual pursuits, delights in reverencing the gods. . .teachers, seniors and elders, is attached to non-violence and is always compassionate, moderate and balanced in his waking and sleeping, is given to regular taking of milk and ghee, is conversant with the science of clime (climate), season and dosage (of foods and herbs), versed in propriety, devoid of egotism, blameless of conduct,

given to wholesome eating, spiritual in temperament
and attached to elders and believers who are self-con-
trolled and devoted to scriptural texts, such a one
should be known as one enjoying the benefits of vitalization therapy constantly. If one who is endowed
with all these qualities makes use of vitalization therapy, that man will realize all the benefits.

Reference to milk and ghee indicates the author's opinion
that they are easily utilized by the body for rebuilding purposes and assist in the circulation of herbal ingredients so
that they are better utilized. Maintaining relationships with
older, wiser people who are models of the ideal life style is
recommended as a supportive influence for one undergoing
rejuvenation procedures.

Two rejuvenation procedures are recommended in Ayurvedic texts: one is for persons who continue their regular
daily routine but who feel the need of internal cleansing and
renewal. I have discussed this program in the preceding chapter. The other is for persons who, out of necessity or because
of choice, undergo the more extreme procedure which requires strict seclusion and the assistance of others.

During his prolonged seclusion the patient-client is visited
by the physician every day and attended by a person who
brings food and toilet articles. Careful attention is given to
progress to ensure that matters proceed smoothly. The patient-
client is given the opportunity to rest completely. Unnecessary
conversation is avoided, no intrusions allowed, and the environment is one of complete isolation. To assist body processes, Hatha Yoga practices may be used and massage may be
administered from time to time. Otherwise, complete rest
and deep meditation are the rule. Rest allows the body to be
renewed and meditation purifies the mind, balances emotions
and introduces fine superconscious forces into the nervous
system.

Some Vitalizing Herbs Used
for Rejuvenation Purposes

Among the wide variety of herbs used for rejuvenation purposes, the mylobalan fruits are highly regarded. These are the *amla* fruit (*Embelica officinalis*); the *harde* fruit (*Terminalia chubulia*); and the *behada* fruit (*Terminalia belerica*). These fruits were plentiful in the area where Mahavatar Babaji once lived and it is known that he made use of them and prescribed their use for others.

Varieties of the Indian gooseberry, mylobalan fruits are small, tart and similar in shape to the kiwi fruit. They are extremely high in Vitamin C content and also contain calcium. While the Vitamin C content may be beneficial, the chief value of the fruits lies in their taste effects upon the governing principles which regulate body functions. Ayurvedic texts cite five of the six tastes as being present in these fruits, while Tibetan medicine declares that they have all six tastes, plus seventeen of the possible medicinal qualities. The seventeen qualities are: soft, heavy, hot, oily, stable, cold, dull, excessively cold, smooth, liquid, dry, dense, light, clear/fragrant/sharp, hard, and fluid. The amla fruit is cooling and tart-tasting. Its name means "sour."

The amla is used when cooling is required, the harde fruit when heating action is indicated, and both are used for combined effects. Both fruits are used along with the behada fruit and mixed with ghee if a lubricating/heating influence is desired, or with honey if a lightening, astringent influence is in order. The amla fruit is also used to make a rejuvenation tonic, still widely appreciated, as a mixture with thirty-four herbs, honey and ghee, then made into a confection. The mixture is heated in water and strained before the honey and ghee are added. This is known as *chayavan prash* and is considered to be a vitalizing mixture.

Another well-known herb is *brahmi* (gotu kola), used to calm mental stress and improve memory. Some believe that its influence is useful in helping to balance the activities between the left and right hemispheres of the brain. This herb is also part of Chinese medicine and is widely known in the

West, as is ginseng, another herb believed to have strengthening and rejuvenating effects on the body. Some herbs such as ginseng should be prescribed according to need if desirable effects are to be realized. With this herb one variety is recommended for men and another for women. It is also frequently prescribed during certain seasons of the year for rejuvenation benefits.

Three special foods are considered to be useful for their cleansing effects as well as for vitalizing the systems of the body. They are garlic, onion and ginger. These "trinity roots" are often taken together to increase their potency, along with clarified butter. Garlic and onion are most potent when taken in raw form but they can also be lightly cooked in clarified butter along with ginger root. The ingredients should be finely chopped before being cooked. Three or four large garlic cloves, one small onion, and about one inch of ginger root can be used for usual purposes. These can be eaten with whole-wheat bread or rice. Larger amounts of garlic are prescribed, prepared in various ways, for extreme rejuvenation procedures. As with other herbs, these should be prescribed according to the basic constitutional nature of the client-patient after a thorough diagnostic examination has been made. Since these foods are somewhat rajasic and tamasic in influence they are sometimes included in the items to be avoided by persons who are leading celibate lives or who are involved with a regimen which is totally sattvic in character.

Some herbs and metals are listed in Ayurvedic literature as having qualities which can prevent the decay and death of the body, an extreme claim. One such plant is *soma*, the basis for a famous rejuvenation therapy procedure known as *soma rasayana*. The fruits, bulbs and creeping branches of the soma plant are ingested after special preparations have been made. Sometimes only the juice from the bulb of the plant is used. The results are said to cause a complete reconstruction of the physical body.

From about 500 B.C., and reaching a peak around 1100 A.D., research was done in South India to discover subtle ways to achieve physical immortality. The procedures are detailed in a system known as *rasashastra*, the main text of which is attributed to a saint known as Siddha Nagarjuna. In one of the texts, the *Jnana Sunkalini Tantra*, is found these words:

> The properties and energies of nature are combined in the rasashastra preparations. The use of pure gold as a catalyst represents the immortality of the self. By the use of rasashastra, properly prepared and purified minerals, the properties and energies of nature within each individual may be rebalanced.

Rasashastra has long since been incorporated into Ayurvedic procedures, and recently more intensive research has begun to determine why these procedures are effective. Since the governing principles are influential even in minerals and metals they have been classified according to these influences. Gold is considered to have a sweet taste and to restore all three governing principles to a condition of balance. It is also described as beneficial to eyesight. Silver is described as acid in taste and cooling to the systems, subduing both Fire and Air governing principles in the body. Copper is said to be astringent in taste and possess qualities which liquify. Iron generates lightness and subdues Fire and Water governing principles. Zinc and lead are said to have a salty taste and, among other influences, are used to expel parasites from the intestinal tract.

Metals used for internal purposes are subjected to lengthy processes of oxidation and "pre-digestion" to remove toxic or harmful effects.

Gems, too, are used for their subtle influences upon the mind and body. Pearls, coral, diamonds and lapis lazuli, for instance, are believed to be cooling in their effects, emotionally calming and beneficial to sight. Extensive literature is available in which the use of gems is prescribed for their direct action upon the body as well as for regulating planetary influences which might contribute to imbalance of the governing principles of the body. Sometimes gems are used along with metals and herbal remedies.

An involved preparatory process results in an acclaimed vitalizing compound known as *makaradhwaja*. I first heard of this rasayana from a brother disciple in 1950. He had heard of an alchemist in southern California who knew its secret and had asked our guru, Paramahansa Yogananda, about it. Paramahansaji knew of the person and of the process but did not encourage the disciple to pursue his investigations at that time.

Makaradhwaja is a combination of mercury purified through several stages of heating, after which sulfer is added, as well as gold; the entire mixture is then heated many times. Without the addition of gold the mixture is known as *rasa-sindura*, and it is used to reduce the Water governing principle in the body, while the mixture containing gold is maka-radhwaja and is used as a general vitalizer. Stories are told of persons living thousands of years as a result of using this preparation.

In Ayurveda, natural substances are prescribed, including foods, herbs, metals and gemstones, for the purpose of balancing the governing principles as well as for regenerating and enlivening the systems. The enlivening or vitalizing procedures are for the purpose of increasing the activity of the vital forces in the body. This category includes the use of substances considered to be aphrodisiac in nature. The purpose is not to irritate the reproductive system in order to stimulate inordinate sexual urges, but to enliven the total organism so that all body functions are as nature intended.

While describing various ways to contribute to such ends, one text concludes by stating that one of the most effective vitalizing factors, among all those which are known, is the presence of an attractive and desirable mate. For one who has not chosen a vocation requiring celibacy, a natural and spontanous conjugal relationship is not incompatible with spiritual practices leading to Self-realization. By living a natural life, and by attending to all prescribed duties in the right way, one's internal forces are inclined to flow increasingly inward so that desires and urges which are not in accord with higher purposes are sublimated. Thoughts, emotions and actions which are in conflict with the fulfillment of final purposes are transformed so that thoughts, emotions and actions which are helpful to the full development of one's inner nature become increasingly evident and influential.

The Ultimate Purpose of Conscious Living

Conscious living enables the soul to experience unbounded awareness and to fulfill its destined purpose of liberation of consciousness. While various therapeutic procedures are offered to persons in all walks of life, to enable them to be healthier and happier, the underlying ideal is to provide them with the opportunity to unfold their divine capacities. Perfected masters are not overly concerned with merely contributing to a continuation of a society which is grounded in conditioned human interests; they desire, instead, that the stream of evolution be assisted in the direction of planetary transformation and world enlightenment.

This should also be our emphasis as we continue through space and time. Whatever we learn which can be useful to us in furthering soul purposes and the divine purpose, should be welcomed. Preoccupation with procedures and practices which but further bind us to *samsara*, endless change, should be renounced. The ideal is to experience changelessness, pure consciousness beyond the relative occurrences of the manifest spheres of Consciousness.

SEVEN

Gemstone, Metal and Color
Radiations as Therapeutic Agents

In Ayurveda, gemstones and metals, because they represent condensed rays of cosmic force, are sometimes used as therapeutic agents. Ayurvedic specialists are not alone in taking this approach, since these natural substances have been used by students of the esoteric sciences of many cultures throughout history.

All material forms emit characteristic radiations due to their contained energy streaming out into surrounding space. Objects are constantly, slowly disintegrating, dissolving, as a result of this process. Energy forms as gross material substances and then gradually flows back to the original formless state. Energies have specific frequencies, according to how they are modified, controlled and directed by the intelligence in nature which coordinates internal processes.

Gem and metal radiation is believed to be received into the body, through the skin, when such materials are worn as body adornment, as jewelry or for specific purposes. Some texts assert that the radiations are transferred to the lymphatic fluids, then to the blood plasma which contains conductive chemicals called electrolytes, in solution. These electrical charges are said to promote the flow of body currents and to affect function.

One conclusion is that gems and metals are formed in the planet as a result of planetary radiations from space acting upon the crystalizing prana of Earth. The one force, flowing into manifestation as the world process, changes into five different frequencies in order to perform the crystalizing, metabolizing, assimilating, circulating and eliminating functions necessary for organic life. The universe is an electrical phenomenon in which forces interact, causing events to take place. According to this perspective, some gems are products of the action of intense heat. Gems and metals are believed to represent the crystalization of ions of elements and element compounds. As essential forms of matter are purified by heat, gems are formed. Some gems grow because of chemical processes, without the presence of intense heat, but the crystalizing influence is still present in the process.

Vedic sources indicate that gems and metals have five primary qualities: the state or effect; the particular attribute, which is either positive, negative or neutral in influence; the power to interact; the interaction itself; and the result of the interaction. Colors as well as chemical composition are considered. Gems are thought of as not only products of planetary radiations but as having the property of being able to attract or repel planetary radiations as well. For this reason only natural gems are recommended for therapeutic purposes when governing principle, and astrological, influences are desired. For color therapy purposes synthetic gems could be prescribed and used.

In Ayurveda, gems and metals have been classified according to their governing principle properties; that is, they are classified according to their Water, Fire or Air influences. Because of this they also impart "taste" influence to the system when utilized in appropriate ways. For instance, ruby has the pungent taste, pearl the astringent taste, coral the bitter taste, emerald has all six tastes, topaz the sweet taste, diamond the sour taste, and sapphire the salty taste. Sweet, sour and salty tastes reduce the Air governing principle; sweet, bitter and astringent tastes reduce the Fire principle; and pungent, bitter and astringent tastes reduce the Water governing principle.

Gems are sometimes administered in the form of ashes

(*bhasmas*), after they have been burned. The fine radiations are still present and are easily absorbed by the body with no toxic side effects.

The more common method is to recommend gems, set in specific metals, to be worn as a ring, a bracelet or a necklace, with an open-backed setting so that radiations can be received directly through the skin.

Gems prescribed to balance the governing principles are selected as foods are selected, for their direct influence on the governing principles of the body. The effects of foods are of short duration, because food is digested rather quickly, while gem and metal effects are more subtle and last longer because their presence is constant as long as they are in proximity to the body. Sometimes gems and metals are worn as a ring, on specific fingers, in order to influence specific body systems through the pranic channels which extend throughout the body and are present at skin surfaces. Gold, for instance, can be worn as a ring on the ring finger to directly influence the reproductive system. Silver, used in this manner, would have a cooling effect.

Metals are "alive," and exhibit signs of wear, stress and fatigue. Some cutting tools, for example, if allowed to rest can be resharpened and will again hold a sharp edge. Research with pyramid energies and moonlight indicates that metal razors respond to energy radiations and will maintain a sharp cutting edge or become dulled depending upon the type of radiation used. Metals disintegrate with age, wear, crumble, and break. Gold, silver and other metals have been used for therapeutic purposes by practitioners of Western medicine. One test indicated that aspirin infused with copper was more result-producing for certain purposes than was aspirin used without the copper present.

A popular method used for the selection of gems to wear as jewelry is to consider the month of one's birth. This is a general approach, rather than for specific purposes. In this method, garnet is considered the stone for January, amethyst for February, bloodstone for March, diamond for April, agate for May, pearl for June, ruby for July, sapphire for August, moonstone for September, opal for October, topaz for November and ruby for December.

Gems are also said to influence the pranas of the body and, through them, the subtle senses. For instance, sight is ruled by the color red, smell by green, touch by violet, sound by blue, and taste by orange. The pranas are ruled in the following ways: vital prana by green; upward prana by violet; even prana by red and yellow; diffused prana by blue; and downward prana by orange and indigo. When pranic frequencies are balanced, health and function are assured.

Cosmic Influences in
Which We Participate

Astrology, along with medicine, mathematics, music and architecture, was one of the great sciences of the ancient world. It was known to Vedic seers, the Chaldeans, Egyptians, Chinese, Persians and the leaders of the past civilizations of the Americas. Astrology is divisible into two distinct emphases. The esoteric science of astrology deals with the mysteries of the cosmos, the spiritual, intellectual, moral and physical chemistry of the world. It reveals the anatomy and psychology of the cosmic processes, setting forth an explanation of existence and pattern of creation and constituting a study of celestial dynamics. Exoteric astrology, on the other hand, is the predictive aspect which is more widely known and more appealing to the general population.

In order to properly understand astrology we must also understand the nature of man, the Spirit-mind-body being. We must also understand the whole of creation, both visible and invisible, that which is seen and that which can only be known subjectively.

In space there are stars, and each star is a self-luminous sun; these suns manifest the pure energy which sustains the worlds. Some suns are orbited by planets which are themselves reflectors of the sun's energies. These planets not only reflect, but also distribute solar radiation. Channeled through the planets, the energy is modified and converted into different frequencies.

So-called material bodies are composed of energy, which has a certain emanational power. The physical energies of these elements are referred to as force, and force exercises an influence upon structures which are in proximity to that force. Man on planet Earth receives three kinds of energy: spiritual energy from the sun and planets; physical energy reflected from the planets, and elementary energy from the Earth on which he resides. Superior forces influence inferior forces, and therefore lesser forces are acted upon by greater forces.

As explained in Part Two, the appearance on the planet of plants and organisms, millions of years ago, was the result of the upward-moving force, attracted by the positive pole of cosmic mind. Spiritual forces work through inert material forms, resulting in subtle interactions and life manifestations. A portion of the Godhead regulates all of creation through these streams of force, as the one Life flows through the suns and is modified and channeled through the planets. As the result of inner contemplation and outer observation, ancient seers were able to discover the qualities of force emanating from certain suns, modified by specific planets. They were then able to recognize the relationship of these forces to the behavior of man, as well as to all living things.

Planet Earth consists of a physical body with a series of electric and magnetic fields. We are bound to the sun by subtle cords, or lines of force. It was taught by ancient seers that Earth contains seven electric zones and, therefore, seven degrees of density. The number seven is often mentioned in esoteric literature: we read of seven continents, seven major racial types, seven great orders of life, seven stages leading to maturity, and seven stages leading to Self-realization. The magnetic field of Earth is nourished by the sun. The entire solar system pulsates, and forces circulate, not unlike the circulation in the physical body. Through the sun we are linked to the rest of the cosmos.

The study of correspondences reveals the great truth that all living beings are part of one magnificent pattern. This is the greatest lesson we can learn from the study of astrology.

With proper study, both intellect and intuition become blended in a natural, harmonious manner and man becomes a sage, one who sees clearly without any errors in perception.

The human organism, so wonderfully complex yet harmonious in all of its parts, became the architectural design upon which seers constructed the "Grand Man of the Starry Heavens." The twelve signs of the zodiac were divided into sections of the human frame, so that the entire zodiacal belt was symbolized as a man bent round in the form of a circle, with the soles of his feet placed against the back of his head. Each of the twelve signs of the zodiac occupies thirty degrees of space, making up the three hundred and sixty degrees of a circle.

More depends upon the position, aspect and influence of the sun and moon at birth than upon the other planets of the solar system. The sun and moon are "transmitters" of stellar forces and act as media which cast their gathered or reflected forces into our magnetic atmosphere, harmoniously or discordantly, according to how they are aspected by the rays of the major planets.

One way to select gems for specific purposes is to determine the planetary rulership of the ascendant or "rising" sign at birth, using the sidereal approach to setting up a horoscope. This is to determine the exact placement of the planets in the constellations in relationship to the time and location of the person when birth occurred. This would be the specific birthstone, rather than the one popularly considered so.

Another approach is to prescribe gems and metals after determining which planetary radiations are weak, strong, or disturbed. To increase a weak influence a gem is chosen to supply more influence of that radiation. To neutralize a strong influence gems would be prescribed to neutralize some of the planetary influence. If disturbance was present because of planetary influences gems would be prescribed to harmonize conditions. For these purposes exact carat weights are calculated based on the radiance influence per carat. In this way recommendations are made for one carat or more, depending upon the calculated influences desired. By knowing the ion value of planetary radiations, perfect gemstones can be prescribed because of their known ion influence, either to neutralize planetary effects or to increase them, according to the stones used.

When color influences are prescribed the cosmic rays are determined by examining the gems with a prism, to determine their color emanation, rather than by relying upon visual inspection alone. Thus, ruby is designated as possessing the red cosmic ray, pearl the orange, coral the yellow, emerald the green, moonstone and topaz the blue, diamond the indigo, sapphire the violet, onyx the ultra-violet, and cat's eye the infra-red color radiation.

It is taught that gems can be purified, that is, residual energies of previous wearers removed, by soaking them in salt water for two or three days. Another way is to bury them in the earth for two or more weeks to allow the Earth's magnetic currents to cleanse them.

Tradition has it that gems can be used in the following ways: for healing, use amethyst, bloodstone or pearl; to experience subtle energy effects, use diamond, lapis lazuli or ruby; for creativity use bloodstone or pearl; to calm emotions, use pearl or opal.

The use of talismans and amulets is common among people of almost every culture, sometimes because of once, or presently accepted knowledge, and sometimes because such objects have been found to be effective as placebos to awaken faith in the patient-client. One's deep belief in the usefulness of a procedure can be a powerful cause which can result in the desired effects, whether they be internal or in relationship to circumstances. Many otherwise sophisticated people will wear a favorite item of clothing or a preferred piece of jewelry because they believe it attracts good fortune, or simply because the wearing of it makes them feel better, or more self-confident.

Lahiri Mahasaya was once asked for a copy of his photograph. He advised the recipient to consider the photograph to have protective influence if she believed it did, but that otherwise for her it would be but a common likeness of him. The person later reported an incident in which she and a family member were protected during a storm because of their faith in Lahiri's presence, through his photograph.

Photographs are believed by many to emanate the radiation of the persons or places reproduced on them. Photographs can, at least, be used to assist in establishing telepathic contact with the photographic subject. In this way contact is established because of focused mental concentration.

While specific recommendations are made to meet personal needs, here follows a general idea of how some gemstones are used in relationship to planetary influences.

Sun — Weak sun influence is said to contribute to an anemic condition and a ruby would be prescribed to provide sun influence to the body. Other problems which may result from a weak sun influence are eye difficulties, indigestion, and emaciation.

Moon — Weak moon influence, when aspected by Saturn, is said to contribute to mental instability. A pearl, for orange radiation, would be prescribed to provide needed moon influence. Other symptoms of weak moon influence include diabetes, bladder disease, lack of courage, improper conduct, and weakness in the face of challenge.

Mars — When Mars influence is weak, coral is recommended. Weak Mars influence is said to contribute to liver problems, impure blood, high blood pressure, piles, urinary difficulties, joint diseases, impatience, mental idleness and depression.

Mercury — Emerald is prescribed when Mercury's influence is weak. Problems arising from its weakness are stomach disorders, aversion to food, poor digestion, lack of discrimination, insecurity, childish behavior and telling untruths.

Jupiter — Either topaz or moonstone is recommended to supply Jupiter's influence when it is weak in one's horoscope. Weak Jupiter influence is said to be associated with mental problems, throat problems, liver disorders, swelling of the body, obesity, tumors, miserliness, propensity for lawsuits, germ phobia, and an overdeveloped sense of self-importance as a personality.

Venus — Diamond is recommended to offset a weak Venus influence. Weak Venus influence is said to contribute to diabetes, uterine problems, problems with the male reproductive system, premature aging, idleness, and delusions.

Saturn — Sapphire is recommended to offset a weak Saturn influence. A weak Saturn influence is said to contribute to neuralgic pains, trembling of limbs and body, nerve disease in general, joint pains, mental problems, hysteria, and inappropriate behavior.

Nodes of Moon — In Indian astrology mention is made of weaknesses related to the nodes of the moon, the points the moon reaches in space relative to earth when it intersects its primary movement. If one's systems are influenced by this placement of the moon it is said that the force contributes to rheumatism, suicidal tendencies, asthma, unfounded fears, diseases of the brain and glands, uterine diseases, asthma, and infections. Onyx and Cat's eye, a variety of chrysoberyl, are recommended.

Some yogis recommend the wearing of yellow sapphire, set in silver and worn on the first finger of the right hand, to cool the system when working with kundalini processes. Another recommendation is to begin to wear a gemstone for therapeutic purposes during the waxing phase of the moon.

Further, it is recommended that if a ring, pendant or bracelet is to be prepared for specific purposes, the jeweler should be a spiritually aware person, manufacture the item during ideal astrological circumstances, and infuse it with the potency of mantras. If one's guru advises the wearing of gemstones, no matter who prepares the finished item it will carry the hidden blessing of the guru.

Astrological timing invites the planetary energies present during that time phase to become a part of the talisman, and mantras mentally or audibly chanted also add their influence. Mantras are sounds representing certain cosmic forces, and these forces, because of their frequencies, exhibit characteristic patterns. Iron filings, for instance, when placed on a smooth surface will form geometrical patterns according to any musical sounds prevailing in the immediate environment. The mantra of the divine energy working through nature which is responsible for healing, integration and evolution is *Om Aim Hrim Klim Chamundayai Viyaya*, and its energy field pattern is the *Sri Yantra*. Mantra is the seed sound, and yantra is its energy form. Sri Yantra is contemplated by some yogis in order to acquire insight into the nature of Consciousness. This process must be learned from a qualified guru.

A visually attractive item of jewelry can be made of gold and set with nine gemstones, representing: emerald for Mercury, topaz for Jupiter, diamond for Venus, sapphire for Saturn, ruby for the sun, coral for Mars, pearl for the moon, and onyx and cat's eye for the nodes of the moon. Such a visual reminder of planetary forces could have value as a talisman rather than for the therapeutic value of the stones because, usually, the carat weights are not considered sufficient to contribute much in the way of direct influence.

Alchemists belonging to secret societies in Europe a few hundred years ago were known to engage in research for the purpose of transmuting base metals into gold, and also to study the radiation influences of precious gems. One legendary figure, known as St. Germain, was said to possess knowledge of procedures enabling him to "manufacture" precious gems. He is believed to have lived for centuries and to have been quietly involved with many political, scientific and philosophical groups.

The esoteric significance of transmutation is not related to natural substances, but rather involves internal transformation resulting in the unfolding of divine qualities. The ancient Chinese adepts, like the yogis, were concerned with internal processes which could be used to "accelerate the rhythms of time" and allow to occur in several years what nature might require many more years to bring about. Included among the inner processes are psychological transformation and the destruction of restricting characteristics, pranayama of a high degree of proficiency, and meditation leading to the experience of pure consciousness. It is taught that permanent realization of pure consciousness is the master key to fulfillment of all purposes, both worldly and divine. Thus, the base characteristics of man are refined and purified so that the "gold" of spiritual knowledge is actualized.

Regardless of one's success in mastering the laws of physical chemistry and the known causes of all external effects, if Self-realization is lacking the purpose for our having taken physical birth is missed. When one lives under the influence of the Holy Spirit, by grace, one will be led into the right pathways of life, and to information which will be useful to one's continued unfoldment.

PART FOUR

Meditation Techniques & Life Enhancement Procedures

ONE

Meditation for Personal Growth and Spiritual Awareness

Regular, correct practice of meditation is the most important spiritual practice for any person who sincerely desires to experience inner growth and spiritual awareness. It is not difficult to learn, and it is a natural process for the soul.

The reason many otherwise devoted persons find it challenging, in the beginning stages, is because their attention has been for so long directed outwardly, causing them to be overly involved in sense experience and external relationships. Turning inward to meditate, then, may require patient practice and sufficient self-discipline to enter into the process. Once the procedure is learned and experienced for a few weeks, it becomes easy and enjoyable.

Because of our feeling nature, when we are outwardly directed we are inclined to seek satisfaction through the senses, by experiencing pleasure and by fulfilling desires. This urge to experience pleasure, usually as a result of fulfilling natural desires, has survival value because it inclines us to do those things which make us happy, assure our comfort and enable us to achieve worthy goals. But when we are compulsively driven, because of feelings of insecurity or ego needs, we are inclined to overindulge the senses and strive too hard to cause effects in our world.

Here is a key to remember: since pleasure satisfies, at least temporarily, an inner need that we have, when we intro-

Meditation Hall at CSA Lakemont.

duce the mind to the superior and more refined pleasurable experience of meditation, the mind is then inclined to seek out that more refined pleasure experience and meditation becomes attractive to us.

You will experience this for yourself as you engage in regular meditation practice. You need not question the matter; you need only put the process to the test of personal experience. If you are a beginning meditator, meditate on a regular schedule, without being overly anxious for immediate results, and then examine how you feel and how you function after a few weeks. This alone will be sufficient proof of the usefulness of meditation.

The Practical Benefits
of Superconscious Meditation

Meditation is the process of arranging conditions so that the body can experience deep relaxation, the thought processes can become dormant, and conscious, clear awareness can be experienced.

As a result of correct meditation practice you will experience superconsciousness, in contrast to the usual three states of ordinary waking consciousness, the subconscious state, and unconsciousness. A basic axiom is: "When mental modifications no longer obstruct soul awareness then one is established in Yoga (awareness of the true Self)." Again, "This state of conscious awareness is accomplished by stopping the waves of the heart." Here, *heart* means "essence of being." When we, at the soul level, are still and no impulses are present to stir the mind, we experience conscious, clear awareness.

Meditation is *not* self-hypnosis, mental procedure, unconscious trance, sleep, daydreaming or preoccupation with astral phenomena. Meditation is practiced for the purpose of allowing the meditator to experience soul awareness, after which one can contemplate the inner nature of Consciousness.

There are natural benefits which unfold in the mind and body of the meditator. The mental field is, in time, purified, the brain and nervous system are unstressed and refined, the body is inclined to function more efficiently and the immune system is strengthened. Blood pressure tends to normalize, thoughts become ordered, emotional satisfaction is experienced, intelligence improves and capacity to appreciate life and living is enhanced. Thinking, feeling and behavior are more easily regulated and environmental harmony prevails. By opening the mind to the field of pure consciousness during meditation, the superior influences originating in that field flow into the mind and body to transform and regenerate on all levels. These claims have been made for hundreds of years by advanced meditators and have more recently been confirmed through research at hundreds of independent universities and research centers.

Even if one is not presently motivated in the direction of Self-realization, regular practice of meditation will result in improved function on all levels and an increase in spiritual awareness. Over a period of years one will naturally unfold in the direction of enlightenment, as the result of increasing superconscious forces working at deeper levels of mind and body. Therefore, to introduce increasing numbers of people to the practice of meditation, whatever the purpose for their beginning their practice, will result in a general improvement of mental, physical and social health. This, too, has value in our awakening world.

The Process of
Meditation

Stages experienced during the correct practice of meditation are observable by the meditator. First, there is a calming effect, followed by deep relaxation. Attention then becomes withdrawn and internalized. Thoughts become refined and gradually settle in the mental field, allowing the meditator to experience a state of relaxed creative awareness. This in itself is beneficial to the mind and the systems of the body and is the procedure used today by millions of people who appreciate the "relaxation response" and its corresponding benefits.

How are we to internalize attention and remove it from feelings and thought processes? To attempt to regulate feelings and thought processes through the will alone is virtually impossible. If one is naturally devoted to God, then inward flowing and contemplation will occur easily. But what if we do not feel devotional or inspired every time we meditate? What, then, can be done? There is an easy and time-tested approach to meditation and it is available to everyone. It is the way of *mantra*.

Mantra is a Sanskrit word combining *man*, "thinking principle," and *tra*, "to take beyond." A mantra, then is a sound introduced into the meditation process for the purpose of taking the attention beyond thoughts.

A mantra is not a magic formula; it is not hypnotic, and it does not require initiation into a "mysterious" regimen of practice. It simply attracts attention and leads it to the source of thought, the still level of the mind. But it is not a mental process in that it does not require thinking, nor does it require concentrated effort. To the contrary, it results in almost *effortless concentration*, concentration being defined as one-pointed flowing of attention to the meditation ideal or object of focus.

For persons interested in the relaxation benefits of meditation, a chosen word or phrase can be used. A non-religious person might select, for example, the word *peace*, or *joy*, or *light*, or whatever word feels comfortable to the mind. Then, sitting upright in a steady meditation posture, with attention directed to the spiritual eye and allowing the breathing to occur in a natural rhythm, one would "float" the chosen word in the mind with each exhalation. The word is not mentally recited; it is "listened to" in the mind. If a phrase is used, the procedure is varied slightly. One would then "listen to" the first part of the phrase with inbreathing, and "listen to" the second part of the phrase with outbreathing. For instance, "I am. . .pure consciousness." Or, "Pure consciousness. . .am I."

This would be continued for fifteen to twenty minutes, without effort to cause anything to happen. By remaining involved with the word or phrase, attention is centered so that thinking is not encouraged and mental wandering does not occur.

A devotional person might use the word God, or Christ, or Love—whatever is comfortable. Or a phrase such as, "God is my life. . .God dwells in me." Or "I am the wave. . .God is the ocean." Or, "I am a bubble. . .in the sea of life."

If the chosen word or phrase causes thinking and speculation, then another, more suitable word or phrase should be used. The idea is to rest in a quiet, thoughtless state during meditation.

If a Sanskrit mantra feels comfortable, one can use it the same way as English words or phrases are used. A common mantra is OM, listened to in the mind with each exhaling breath. Or *hong-sau*, listened to with incoming and outflowing breaths. Or *so-hum*, used in the same way.

Once a word, a phrase or a mantra is found which is result-producing, it should remain the one used every time you meditate. In this way you will become familiar with it and, as the result of previous successes with it, it will become "spiritualized" and quickly lead the attention inward whenever you use it.

A single-syllable mantra, such as Om, can be listened to steadily during meditation without attention being given to breathing. This affords the opportunity for deeper meditation, because attention is then also withdrawn from the body and its movements.

A typical meditation session would be as follows:

1. *Sit in an Upright Position* — Flow attention upward to the spiritual eye. This will reverse attention from without to within and encourage an upward flow of body forces and prana. Think of God and feel thankful and receptive, perhaps with a brief devotional prayer. If you want to precede meditation with a few rounds of alternate nostril breathing, to calm body and mind and balance prana flow, do this.

2. *Be Attentive to Natural Breathing* — Just relax into your body and feel the natural rhythm of the body breathing, breathing from the diaphragm to induce relaxation. Begin to introduce the word, phrase or mantra.

3. *Continue with the Process* — As you continue you will become less aware of body motion (due to breathing) and

more involved with inner processes. Assume that the inner sound you use, or hear, has an origin and follow it to that origin. This will lead your attention from gross, to subtle, to fine levels of awareness.

4. *Rest in the Peak Experience* — You will know when you have reached the peak experience, the depth of experience for that particular session. Rest here without the word, phrase or mantra, for as long as you feel comfortable.

5. *Come Out of Meditation* — Open your eyes when you are ready, and rest for a few moments in the stillness. Acknowledge your environment and go about your activities.

For relaxation purposes, the entire session will require fifteen to twenty minutes, or a bit more. For deeper contemplation, if you feel so led, let the session run until you feel right about concluding it.

Meditate once a day, although twice a day would be better. Useful times are early in the morning after awakening, before thoughts and feelings become pronounced due to involvement with the daily routine, and in the evening after the day's activities are concluded. Some meditators find it useful to meditate after work in the evening, prior to the evening meal. Others prefer to meditate at a later hour.

Meditate before eating or after a meal has had time to digest. The reason for this is that meditation slows the body's processes and the process of digestion should not be interfered with by meditation.

Many people experience no difficulty in sleeping after they meditate just prior to bedtime. Others find that meditation causes them to become so aware that sleep does not follow easily. This will have to be determined by the individual meditator, as there can be no firm rule about the matter.

Remember, always, you are meditating to allow yourself to experience your higher nature. You are not meditating to *become* that nature. By inward meditation and contemplation we become increasingly aware of our larger Self as pure consciousness. To the degree that we do this, the field of pure consciousness influences can bring about beneficial changes which contribute to more conscious living.

TWO

How to Experience Creativity and the Completion of Purposes

With increasing awareness, creativity naturally increases. With increasing awareness, there are fewer restrictions in body, mind and consciousness; one is therefore able to fulfill worthy purposes more easily.

Inhibiting mental restrictions may include faulty beliefs about the rightness or wrongness of actions performed to cause effects, or about the rightness or wrongness of expressing success and abundance in this world. These are often major internal barriers for devotees on the enlightenment path, especially those who are concerned with avoiding future complications which might interfere with Self-realization.

Let us clearly understand that nature is Consciousness, manifesting *as* nature. When we can perceive without errors we can function in this world without creating problems for ourselves or for others. Man is a goal-achieving being because it is his nature to be intelligently involved with the life process. All of our actions should be implemented for the purpose of fulfilling duties, accomplishing purposes and assisting the trend of evolution in the direction of fulfillment. With these ideals in mind we are not likely to be self-serving, manipulative or prone to making errors in judgment or behavior.

It is the responsibility of every awakened person to consciously come to terms with the manifest world and to function in it with understanding. To avoid this responsibility is to shirk duty and to fail in the purpose for having been born here. A fearful, cowardly person is unlikely to be successful on the spiritual path because he is unwilling to confront reality at this or any other level.

With total enlightenment one experiences a complete absence of restrictions. Between ordinary human states of consciousness and the level of full enlightenment, however, various restrictions prevail. Therefore, with increasing awareness many restrictions are removed or transcended, and with increasing success in relating to the world in an intelligent manner, enlightenment unfolds more easily and quickly. We can consider our tour of duty in this world as a learning opportunity, a school of higher education, and an opportunity to test and prove the principles we learn.

In yogic texts are to be found descriptions of soul capacities which can unfold as fewer and fewer restrictions remain, as a result of awakening. Within range of almost everyone is the ability to learn to live in harmony with natural laws and experience health, function and all of the creature comforts necessary for a peaceful life. It requires little in the way of study and application to see to these circumstances, as evidenced by the millions of people in the world who are experiencing them. Even those who are not consciously on the enlightenment path are often able to satisfy their basic urges and accomplish their major purposes. More enlightened people should be able to do these things easily, and more.

An enlightened person can often do things which ordinary people consider to be supernatural, yet they are as natural to such a person as ordinary circumstances are to the average person. This is because an enlightened person sees from a different vantage point: he sees from the realm of higher consciousness, and he knows that the material universe is but manifesting effects of inner, more subtle causes.

Stories are told of how enlightened men and women can control the weather, attract anything they want into their lives, heal others with a thought or by intention, see into the heart of an atom, know what is occurring many miles distant, even levitate the body—in short, do whatever they want to do because they recognize no limitations at all. We read of how saints transform matter, materialize food and other objects, and call life back into a body that has ceased to function. Is it only the masters who have these abilities? Or is it that they know something that many do not?

Yes, it is that they know something. They know who they are, they know the nature of Consciousness, and they are not restricted by thoughts, beliefs or circumstances. They work with natural laws, but from the level of higher understanding. They see through matter to the field of light and the realm of primal substance, and they think and function from there.

Many texts dealing with enlightenment procedures warn against the use of soul abilities because of the possiblity that one who is overly fascinated by them will misuse them or forget the higher goal of life. This is good advice. It does not mean, however, that we should not use our natural abilities, with understanding, to accomplish useful purposes. The major injunction is not to be caught up and fascinated with these processes and not to misuse them because of egotistical involvement with life.

A responsible person is not going to get off the path, is not going to forget the goal of Self-realization, is not going to be driven by need, pride or selfishness. A responsible person is going to attend to his duties, live a moral life, become increasingly God-conscious and be open to inner guidance. Such a person will then rightly use his soul abilities. The "kingdom of heaven" is sooner or later going to manifest on earth, and the more conscious people there are who live without restrictions the sooner it will unfold. So, if you plan to be a citizen of the New era, where harmony prevails and all suffering is eliminated, perhaps you had better seriously think about growing into maturity and getting on with the business of learning your way around the universe—and this includes learning how to function right where you are in the highest and best way. Small-minded, fearful, dependent people are unlikely to be able to enjoy the New Era. They will either be forced to awaken and mature, or they will have to fulfill their destiny elsewhere. The cosmic life force will have its way with the evolutionary process.

Four Ways of Contributing to the Completion of Purposes

Depending upon our level of understanding, we do our work and we experience the completion of worthy purposes. If purposes are not worthy of you, renounce them. Establish your priorities and be engaged in only worthy activities and projects.

1. *The Way of Most Effort* — This is common to the average unawakened person. It is the way of working hard, exchanging time and energy for desired results. There is nothing demeaning about honest hard work; the only problem with working all of the time at this level of understanding is that results are limited to what one can do in a given time. Even working at peak capacity for fifteen or more hours a day, seven days a week, one could only earn the equivalent of time and energy expended.

2. *The Way of Less Effort* — Being willing and able to work at a steady pace, one at this level also utilizes possibility-thinking to solve problems, improve performance, eliminate waste motion, and to harness machines and other labor-saving devices in order to multiply efforts. One would also invest income, enter into cooperative relationships with others and, in short, use executive abilities to improve performance and learn how to utilize existing forces (including nature's forces) in a more productive way. The same amount of time and energy may be utilized in this way, but the results are dramatically increased.

3. *The Way of Least Effort* — Along with creative endeavors one would, after meditation, learn to visualize goals as being "now" achieved and purposes as being "now" fulfilled. In this way, using creative imagination and adjusting the inner state of consciousness, one could encourage the unfoldment of creative ideas and actually attract into his life

the very circumstances envisioned. This is a higher level of creativity, the level from which one inwardly sees "ends" instead of beginnings and learns to work in harmony with cosmic mind, which is responsive to our thoughts and our assumptions..

4. *The Way of No Effort* — Here one does whatever feels right and flows with life. Because of being consciously aware of his real nature, and his relationship with the one Life, he is in the flow of grace. Whatever he needs flows to him without effort. The reason for this is that when we are established in God-consciousness, if anything disturbs our inner equilibrium, be it a just desire or a need that unfolds, the force of the universe will satisfy the desire or meet the need in order to restore us to equilibrium. This is why a person in this state finds that even small desires and whims are satisfied.

Whatever life experience we can believe ourselves worthy of, and can accept, if it can be arranged by nature, we can experience it. Things not yet created can be created, machines not yet invented can be invented, solutions to problems can unfold, circumstances can change. All things, in harmony with natural law, are possible. Therefore, think in terms of fulfillment on all levels and do not settle for failure, limitation or restriction in any area of your life. You are here to glorify God.

1. *Self-Realization* — Accept Self-realization as the natural unfoldment of soul destiny and do all you can to allow yourself to experience it.

2. *Harmony with Cosmic Mind* — Through your thinking, believing and knowing, you can enter into a cooperative working relationship with cosmic mind, the mind of God. The principles are easy to learn and to apply. All it requires of us is practice.

3. *Emotional Maturity* — This comes down to one thing— our willingness to be self-responsible for our states of consciousness, our thoughts, feelings and behavior, what we have done in the past, what has happened to us, what we will do in the future and, in brief, our total relationship with life.

4. *Physical Health and Function* — Your body is the "temple of the Holy Spirit," the life of God. It can be healed, if need be, and it can be enlivened and made radiant with the light of the soul.

5. *Harmony with Nature* — The universe is supportive and benevolent. When we are on "friendly terms with a friendly world" we find that nature is our friend and will support us in every way.

6. *Prosperity and Fulfillment of Purposes* — To prosper is to thrive, to flourish and to be successful in all useful ways. Life's inclination, as evident about us in nature, is to thrive, to flourish and to be successful, that is, to fulfill intended purposes. You, too, should thrive, flourish and be fulfilled. In this way no lack is experienced and you become a conduit through which Spirit performs useful services in this world.

I am writing out of my own experience as I share these thoughts with you. I grew up in a rural community, during the years following the Great Depression in America, and I experienced lack and limitation. I also experienced a severe illness. Later, for almost four years, I was fully engaged in spiritual practices and service in a monastic environment. After that I was led to minister around the world, and, over the years, I have learned to live "out of consciousness" and to prove the principles I now share with you. So I am not writing these principles just because I have read about them (although I have read widely); I am speaking of possibilities as the result of personal application and experience. I know these principles are valid. And, because they are principles of mind and consciousness, they will work for any person who will learn to apply them. Furthermore, God's grace will flow through anyone who is surrendered to it. This requires an adjustment in understanding; this is the only key.

Open Yourself to
Infinite Possibilities

Because we are able, when awakened and knowledgeable, to be open to the flow originating in the pure field of consciousness, infinite possibilities are available to us. If we are not used to being open to the flow it will require of us that we enter into willing participation in life and learn, through experience, how to be responsive. From time to time, during a quiet interlude, preferably after meditation, do the following:

1. *Write a List of Your Hopes and Dreams* — Obtain several notebooks and keep them in a private place, for your use alone. During a quiet time, with no inhibitions, write a list of your worthy hopes and dreams, all of the things you would like to do and experience. Certainly you will want to list many of these under the headings of Self-realization, creativity, emotional maturity, physical health and vitality, supportive relationships (with nature and with other people), and aims and purposes (your meaningful goals).

Write clearly what you want to experience in these areas. Write what you will do to make possible the fulfillment of your dreams. Write clearly any obstacles to the fulfillment of your dreams, and what you will do, starting now, to eliminate such obstacles.

While doing this, do not think of limitations. Be open to infinite good and know that you are working in partnership with the power that nourishes the universe. Even if some of your hopes and dreams seem to you to be out of the question, write them clearly anyway. You can always modify your list later, or it may be that you will find that you didn't dream big enough, that life is more than willing and able to fulfill your dreams in spite of your present limitations in thinking and imagining. As you write, remember that if your dreams are useful, if they are worthy of you and of value to others, life can and will bring together the resources and means to embody your dreams. In your heart, as you write, accept the ideal of Self-realization, unlimited creativity, emotional maturity, physical health and vitality, the love and support of your world, and success in all useful ventures. *Writing in this way, with your mind open to the universe, is one of the most important things you can do to assist yourself in the direction of total fulfillment.*

2. *Write a Life Plan* — Contemplate deeply the purpose for which you were born. Why are you here in this world? Never mind, for the moment, what you have done or have not done thus far in your life. Just examine your life and think in terms of what you want to accomplish or experience before you depart from this world. Write your goals and major purposes and resolve to eliminate whatever stands in the way of fulfillment. How many years do you have left in this incarnation? What do you intend to do with the years yet remaining? Be as specific as you can, while remaining open to the unplanned good fortune which will surely unfold in the near and distant future.

Keep your writings where you can refer to them from time to time, and add to what you have written when inspiration unfolds. Make a conscious and honest effort to do all you can do to be a responsible participant in the process of unfoldment and actualization of personal dreams and Self-realization.

A Four-Step Creative Visualization Technique

After meditation, or just before going to sleep at night (or before taking a nap anytime), consciously use this recommended method to adjust your state of consciousness, your outlook on the world and your feelings about yourself and your world.

1. *Rest in the Creative Silence* — If sitting after meditation, remain sitting in a relaxed state of conscious awareness. Out of this state of consciousness "all things are possible." If you are practicing this technique just before going to sleep, then lie down and relax, in a meditative mood. Feel yourself to be a formless unit of pure consciousness.

2. *Specific Mental Imagery* — Visualize, in your mind's eye, yourself as you want to be, as: enlightened, functional, healthy, happy, successful and free. It may be that you will want to just do this, and allow everything else to unfold in natural order. Or it may be that you feel led to be specific

and visualize yourself in circumstances which would reflect your dream or desire as fulfilled.

3. *Feel Your Ideal State and Circumstances to be Real* — Bring your mental work into the realm of feeling and *feel* the reality of your desired state of consciousness and your desired circumstances. Do not think of future-time possibilities; feel your dream or desire to be a *now* reality. Embody it in your consciousness and feeling.

4. *Rest in the Realization* — Rest in the mood of realization until it is the only reality you know, then emerge from the practice session and retain that state of consciousness and that feeling. If practicing before sleep, once established in the mood, go to sleep and seal that state of consciousness within you.

Once you are inwardly established in the new state of consciousness, what you are, as consciousness, must unfold on the screen of space and time. It is impossible for it to be otherwise because the spiritual law is that consciousness creates outer reality.

There will often be a time factor to consider. It may require the passage of time for internal psychological and body changes to occur, if you have been working to create such changes. It may require the passage of time for outer circumstances to change, or for events to come together, if you have been working to modify your personal world, including your relationships. Just remember, once you have sealed the new state of consciousness and it is permanent, fruits must unfold. The seed is your new state of consciousness, and the harvest is the outer effect.

If you can do something, and you often can, to participate in the process by allowing unfoldment of circumstances, do what you can. If you have done all you know to do, then be firm in inward realization and allow life to make whatever arrangements are necessary to embody your dream.

Out of your own field of consciousness, impulses will flow which will have corresponding effects in the relative world.

Your clear thought images will meld with the field of cosmic mind and cosmic mind will externalize your thought images.

As you use this technique you are the observer and the one who experiences. You are not the doer. Therefore, learn to avoid too much personal involvement and be thankful to life for all unfoldments. By too much personal involvement I mean, do not become selfishly attached, either to the process or to the results. In this way you will always remember that you are cooperating with the power that runs the universe, but that you are not the master of the universe. And, always, before entering into any creative process, pray for guidance so that you are led from within to make wise choices. When others are involved, always think of their highest and best and never think in terms of competition or exploitation. Paramahansaji used to say that the world is big enough for everyone, that there is room for everyone to fulfill his purposes without anyone having to be deprived.

It is Our Duty to
Prosper in All Ways

If we are not open to the flow of life we deprive ourselves of the opportunity to fulfill our purposes. To be affluent means to be in the flow of creative thoughts, ideas, and all that is required to express freely and righteously. One might experience a flow of creative ideas but seldom benefit as a result and, therefore, prosperity would not manifest. Or one might possess many things but be possessed by them, and this is not being prosperous. To have at hand what we need to accomplish worthy purposes is to be prosperous.

The primal substance of nature is limitless and is always changing form. Food, clothing, houses, automobiles, books, money, everything formed of this primal substance, is just this substance formed as we see and use it. To be prosperous, look to the source, and out of the source all forms will flow into your life as you need them. This is what it means to be truly prosperous.

Cultivate a prosperity consciousness, an attitude of limitlessness. Nothing belongs to you, or to anyone; everything is provided by life for our convenience. To use resources wisely is an indication of spiritual and emotional maturity. To misuse resources is destructive, and to back away from useful involvement, when the need is present, is to avoid our obvious duty.

Practice of meditation, using the technique for listening to the inner sound, while feeling oneness with all of nature, is a useful process for the purpose of becoming consciously attuned to the forces of the universe. What "we ask for" while immersed in the Aum current is certain to unfold. Even if we do not ask, whatever is needed by us will unfold because of grace.

To be more in the flow of good be attentive to giving to life, giving not from yourself, but from the source within you which is the same as the source of everything. Realize that everything in nature unfolds from the source into manifestation. You cannot be depleted when you give from the source because it has endless capacities to express and manifest.

The moment you give, in the way of service, or good thoughts, or a supportive word, in the form of money or other things of a practical nature, you are blessed because you are in the flow. Giving in this way does not bind you to the wheel of causation, to cause and effect. You are not, then, giving in order to receive; you are giving from the source which can never be depleted. Therefore, the moment you give, rightly, you are in the stream of endless blessings.

To continue to prosper, continue to give with the understanding that you are distributing the substance of God. You are not giving anything of your own and, therefore, when you give wisely you will not feel disappointed if your giving is not appreciated and you will not need personal recognition for your giving. You will know that you are not the giver, but merely the steward, the responsible distributor of supporting substance.

If you are in a guru-disciple relationship, support your guru's mission with your prayers, thoughts, words, actions and resources. If you attend a church, support your church in the same way. Give also to worthy community projects, and to whatever will assist society to function and be more healthy. Help those who need help, support educational systems, the arts and research projects. If you are on the enlightenment path, let the major portion of your efforts be in the direction of providing enlightenment services to seeking souls.

Do not assert that you have nothing to give. Of course you have nothing to give—but the ocean of life is all around you and you can give from that source. You can draw upon it to meet your own needs and you can channel it to others for their welfare and for the welfare of humanity.

Let the work you do, for enjoyment or for compensation, be true service. If you are on the enlightenment path do not waste your time and energy doing what a machine could do better, and do not engage in activities which are not life-enhancing and health-producing for others. Let the ideal of sattvic, uplifting influence be evident in everything that you do and, in this way, be totally involved with constructive activities. This is the true way to prosperity and conscious awareness of God. This realization will assure your freedom of expression in all planes and spheres.

If You Need Healing, Do These Things Now

If there is dis-ease or lack of ability to function without restrictions, at any level of life experience, you are in need of healing. Carefully study the material in this book, especially the section on health, healing and radiant living, and implement a program right away to put an end to your troubles. Do all of the practical things which seem useful to you while living from the inner awareness of the soul. Be reminded that our life experiences flow from our states of consciousness.

If you need assistance, see your spiritual mentor or a competent person who will be able to help you. Even minor inner or outer disturbance can later result in major problems, so remove even minor disturbances. Use this approach:

1. *Sit in the Silence After Meditation* — Feel yourself dissolve in pure consciousness. Sit for as long as you need to in

order to arrive at this level of awareness, and remain in it for a long time.

2. *Inwardly Know Perfection* — Know that you are made in the image and likeness of God, that you are a ray of pure consciousness. Know, because of this, that you cannot experience imperfection. Experience wholeness and completeness— as a being, at the mental level, at the emotional level, at the body level, and in relationship to your world. Know only wholeness, completeness and right action.

3. *Rest in This Knowing* — There is no need at this time to attempt to find solutions for problems or to accomplish anything. Just rest in this knowing until you are completely absorbed in knowing.

4. *Emerge from the Session Renewed* — You are now "in your right mind" in that you are now anchored in the realization of who you are and what your relationship with God is. Healing forces will awaken as a result, if you have been in need of physical healing, and your body will be renewed. Any mental, psychological, physical or circumstantial inharmony will be restored to harmony. Inwardly know, "Everything in my consciousness, everything in my mind, everything in my world, is now in divine order." Feel thankful and rejoice!

To pray for others who may have asked you for healing of any kind, take them into meditation, in your own mind and consciousness, and give them to God. See perfection for them. Know that the activity of the Holy Spirit is active through and around them, now, and is moving in the direction of spiritual unfoldment, appropriate transformation, needed changes and completion. Just know this totally within yourself, on their behalf. Release it and be thankful.

If appropriate, with others as with yourself, provide any needed support to assist the healing process. Merely praying for ourselves, or for others, is useful but often not enough for final results. What is often needed is education, so that we clearly understand the nature of Consciousness and the laws of nature. In this way, after healing one will never have major problems of any kind in the future.

Utilize any of these processes according to need and inner guidance until you become proficient in their use. Then, at any time when you feel the need, you will know what to do and how to do it. You will increasingly actualize all of your soul capacities and be a true representative of God's will.

THREE

The Philosophy and Practice
of Kriya Yoga

A superior and result-producing meditation technique, suitable for persons in our current time cycle, is the technique known as *Kriya Yoga* pranayama. The Sanskrit root of *kriya* is *kri*, to do, to work. Kriya Yoga is, then, a process which enables the meditator to experience unity consciousness with God.

I was initiated into Kriya Yoga by my guru, Paramahansa Yogananda, in the summer of 1950. After the group initiation ceremony, he placed his hands upon my head and taught me how to see the inner light at the spiritual eye. As I looked within, both of us directing our gaze inward, I beheld a clear silvery white orb against the background of a dark blue field. He said to me, "That light is Krishna and Radha, Spirit and nature. Now, you can see that light any time when you do this."

The philosophy and practice of Kriya Yoga has been known for many centuries, and the basic text outlining the philosophical basis for practice is the Yoga Sutras of Patanjali. Patanjali, a seer who lived many hundreds of years ago, compiled the information and wrote the basic precepts in the form of *sutras*, concise aphorisms to be contemplated for their inner meaning. The two basic texts recommended to all Kriya Yoga practitioners are the Yoga Sutras and the Bhagavad Gita. The former outlines, in systematic style, the way to concentration, meditation and Self-realization. The latter offers philosophical information and basic guidelines for living a God-centered life. Both works mention pranayama as a way to still the mental waves in order to experience release from bondage to the mind and senses. In the Yoga Sutras, we read (2:49—52):

> When the meditation posture is mastered, then the circulation of gross vital forces ceases. The modifications of pranayama are either external, internal, or motionless. They are long or short and modified by space, time and number. Another modification of pranayama is that of neutralizing inhalation and exhalation. As a result of mastery of pranayama the darkness which veils the light of the soul is removed.

From the Bhagavad Gita (4:28, 29):

> Some devotees offer as sacrifice their material possessions, their self-discipline or their spiritual exercises, while others of subdued minds and strong determination and resolve offer their learning and knowledge. Others, again, who are devoted to life force control, having restrained the movements of the alternating flow of vital force in the body, neutralize the flow and rise above body and mind into the awareness of Transcendental Being.

By the correct practice of Kriya Yoga pranayama, the meditator takes in an extra supply of prana and neutralizes decay processes in the body. The heartbeat slows, breathing slows, and internal systems are balanced. With the balancing of internal pranas, the mental waves become dormant and inner awareness unfolds spontaneously.

Breathing, the motions of prana in the body, and mental modifications are interrelated. When a person is intently concentrating, internal pranas are synchronized and breathing is automatically regulated. In reverse order, to calm the mind a direct approach is to regulate the breathing rhythm by prac-

ticing Kriya Yoga pranayama. In this way one is able to immediately acquire control over internal pranas and, thereby,
mental processes.

Although the Kriya process is known by various names
(and practiced by many with certain modifications), the technique as taught through the line of gurus tracing back through
Paramahansaji, Sri Yukteswar, Lahiri Mahasaya and Mahavatar
Babaji is the one shared here. Babaji himself said that he but
restored the practice in modern times, after it had been "forgotten" during the last Dark Age cycle. During the Dark Age
it was known to only a few spiritual masters and it was not
widely taught because few aspirants were qualified to understand and utilize it. In 1861 Lahiri Mahasaya met his guru,
Mahavatar Babaji, in northern India in the Himalayan foot-
hills, and he was instructed in the ancient procedure. Lahiri
was given permission to initiate others after carefully assessing
their spiritual capacities and intentions on the path.

One of Lahiri's advanced disciples, Sri Yukteswar, trained
Paramahansaji for his mission to the West. I have told about
these masters and the transmission of the Kriya Yoga tradition
in my books, *God Has Given Us Every Good Thing* and *The
Science of Kriya Yoga.* Paramahansaji first shared knowledge
of the Kriya Yoga path in his book, *Autobiography of a Yogi.*

The Kriya Yoga path includes more than the practice of
the pranayama and related meditation techniques. It embraces
the totality of one's life, with emphasis upon living in accord
with the precepts ordained to enable one to live in harmony
with natural and spiritual laws. Babaji, for instance, instructed
Lahiri to give Kriya initiation only to those who offered their
lives to God, and who were honest in their dealings and completely responsible in their personal relationships. Lahiri, too,
often refused to instruct disciples into higher meditation procedures until after they had mastered the preliminary ones,
and then only if they were fulfilling their family and social
duties in the right way. Kriya Yoga is not for escapists who
mistakenly think that they have but to practice meditation
while ignoring other responsibilities which have been assumed
at birth, and which have been accepted as commitments.

Kriya Pranayama: Technique
for Accelerating Transformation

Vedic seers have long taught that ordinary man's spiritual evolution is related to the soul's ability to express through the mind and body. While the soul is pure consciousness, as long as it is identified with the mind and body it is restricted, because of the many acquired conditionings and limitations. The removal of these conditionings and limitations is the purpose of certain spiritual practices. As the result of such practices they are resisted, restrained, and finally dissolved, thus allowing the light of the soul unobstructed radiance.

Further, it is taught that subtle changes take place in the human body, including the nervous system and brain, due to nature's influences. Not only the nourishing characteristics of the sun, fresh air, pure water and natural food, but harmonious surroundings and emotional and mental peace also contribute to the transformation of the body and internal aspects: the astral sheath, causal sheath and mental field. There is another influence, also—the attracting magnetic influence of God. While this attracting influence unveils soul capacities, it also contributes to subtle transformation of body, subtle organs, and mind.

In the Kriya Yoga tradition it is taught that the human body is replenished every year, which includes a little more than twelve lunar months, and that every twelve years, all external and internal conditions being ideal, obvious transformational changes take place which propel us along the evolutionary path.

What the Kriya practitioner does, by directing life force through the spinal pathway (*sushumna*, the "path of God"), is to do for himself what nature does for him over a longer period of time. Sri Yukteswar once said to Paramahansaji, "Kriya Yoga is an instrument through which human consciousness can be quickened. The ancient yogis discovered that the secret of cosmic consciousness is intimately linked with breath mastery. The life force, which is ordinarily absorbed in maintaining heart action, must be freed for higher activities by a method of calming and stilling the ceaseless demands of the breath."

In effect, what nature does over thousands and millions of years in the way of transforming the body and inner organs of experience and perception is accomplished by the person practicing Kriya Yoga pranayama in only several years. It must be remembered that not all persons begin their spiritual quest from the same level of consciousness. Some are already more advanced in knowledge and awareness. However, regardless of one's present status, practice of Kriya techniques can be helpful.

During the practice of Kriya pranayama, through inward concentration and the use of a certain breathing method, the meditator is able to draw life force up through the spinal pathway, into the brain, and then let it flow down in reverse order. With the body relaxed, and due to deeper breathing, extra oxygen received by the body is transmuted into prana and used to magnetize and regenerate the spinal nerves and brain tissues.

There is a relationship between enlightenment and physiology. People whose brains and nervous systems are unrefined can hardly manifest the force of Spirit through the body until transformation occurs. This is why time is built into the unfolding process. It requires the passage of time for internal changes to occur. True, through devotion and commitment one may experience a degree of spiritual awareness, and even undergo a dramatic conversion experience during which internal changes result which are quite dramatic. But in these instances, the physiology is already somewhat refined and responsive to higher frequencies of consciousness.

Through right living, right diet, right thinking, right behavior, and deep meditation sattvic influences contribute to inner transformation of the body and subtle nature so that it is easier for soul awareness to unfold.

We must avoid one major error, however, the error of believing that it must require many, many years for enlightenment to be experienced. It is possible to experience pure consciousness during meditation and to experience the infusion

of superconscious forces which greatly contribute to the refinement of the mental field, brain, nervous system and body.
The increase of fine spiritual force, *ojas*, as the result of right
living and superconscious meditation, is the most influential
ingredient of all.

I mention this because I have known many, even some on
the Kriya Yoga path, who have fallen into the habit of thinking
that they are sentenced to years of hard work before they
can expect obvious results from their practice. Or they often
judge others on the path by how long they have been engaged
in spiritual practices and meditation. The belief that "it will
take years, or incarnations, to attain the spiritual goal" is a
self-defeating one.

Another self-defeating attitude results from the mistaken
opinion that others, if they are not practicing the procedures
that we practice, have a more difficult and longer way to go.
It is impossible, except for a true spiritual master, to know
another's inner condition or what his destiny is on the path.

The Kriya Yoga path is for persons who feel drawn to it,
who are able to understand the basis for it, and who are willing
to practice until desired results are experienced. Even a Kriya
practitioner must avoid thinking that he is special because of
his knowledge, or that he is superior to others whose path
may be different.

We should not believe that, because we are practicing
these techniques, we are in any way improving upon our soul
nature. All we are doing is contributing to our ability to transcend restricting influences, including mental modifications,
and working to transform the body and inner nature so that
increasing degrees of soul awareness can freely express through
mind and body.

Kriya pranayama is traditionally taught during an occasion of private instruction. This is the occasion of initiation.
During this encounter the guru, or a representative of the
guru, explains the procedure and observes the initiate in order
to be assured that the instruction is understood. This is the
occasion when the new initiate commits himself to the spiritual path without reservations. In this way the transmission

of the technique remains pure and the initiate is assured that proper transmission has occurred. The technique, because of its intricate character, cannot be learned from a book or from someone who knows about it but who has not experienced deep and prolonged practice of it.

The beginning Kriya meditator is advised to practice fourteen times once or twice a day. The reason for this is that one is attempting to accomplish, at subtle and gross levels, what nature accomplishes during the solar year. By concentrating at the spiritual eye, with attention focused in the spinal pathway and brain, using the prescribed breathing method, one circulates life current up and down the spine. The crown chakra represents the inner sun, and the mind represents the moon. The mind is refreshed and cleansed as attention, with life current, is circulated through the spinal pathway during Kriya pranayama. Also cleansed are the subtle channels (*nadis*) through which prana circulates. Kriya, then, is a cleansing process. This is why, even if little in the way of progress in meditation is experienced, one should continue to practice Kriya pranayama, as duty, without expectation of immediate results.

Advanced Practice
of Kriya Pranayama

After one has been faithful in the practice of Kriya pranayama for several months to a year, doing fourteen cycles per session twice a day, one can increase to twenty-eight or fifty-six times. It is usual to increase in multiples of fourteen, this number being prescribed to insure thirteen cycles, the equivalent of the number of lunar months in one solar year. (Some teach that each revolution, ascending and descending, is the equivalent of one solar year, but this would depend upon the depth of experience.) Paramahansaji taught us that the deeper the practice the more result-producing was our practice. He always stressed depth of practice, as well as the recommended number of pranayamas.

After regular practice over a period of time, one will notice that the inner currents circulate of their own accord during the day. They may even become continuous, although usually one will feel them surge more strongly during some times of the day and then subside for a duration. These surges of creative current are directed by an inner intelligence and they will work according to the need and capacity of the individual.

As the initiate progresses the guru will advise as to when to increase the practice and give instructions of a personal nature as required. Some advanced practitioners increase the number of cycles by meditating more than twice a day. Some meditate morning, noon and evening. Others add still another session at midnight. Dawn, noon, dusk and midnight are times when subtle changes occur in nature, during transition phases, and these are believed to be useful times to meditate for the purpose of harmonizing inner processes.

Assuming two meditation sessions per day, during which one practiced fourteen cycles at each session (to accomplish thirteen complete ones) one would, in one day, experience the equivalent of two years of natural evolution, or seven hundred and thirty years in twelve months. Assuming each cycle to be the equivalent of one year, for more in-depth practice, one would accomplish the equivalent of over nine thousand years of inner evolutionary influence. By intensifying his practice, one could accomplish in one life cycle what nature takes one million years to effect.

There have been a few advanced practitioners who have performed over a thousand cycles a day for several years and who have become highly advanced spiritually. On the other hand, there are some who become proficient in practice, and are inwardly awake to a degree, but who have not been able to renounce their attachment to formal practices or their rigid attitudes about philosophical matters. An attitude of self-righteousness and "pride of attainment" has prevented many an advanced yogi from surrendering to grace. There are many almost illumined souls who roam the various spheres as gods who could yet learn much from simple devotees who have inwardly given their lives to God.

Some who have progressed on the Kriya path have, after

months or years of dedicated practice, fallen away because of lack of sustained devotion, failure to be regular in practice, or because of becoming involved with modifications of the mind. Others have continued with their practice but have become caught up in internal and external phenomena and neglected to adhere to the basic advice, which is to renounce all that stands in the way of final realization.

During meditation, for instance, the meditator's attention may falter and be drawn into involvement with memory, causing him to dwell on past incidents or to be overcome by the pressures of emotion welling up from the subconscious. Or one may inwardly perceive a variety of subtle manifestations— lights, sounds and visions— which are constantly changing, and become overly fascinated with such transitory phenomena. There is the possibility, too, of experiencing hallucinations manufactured by the mind, either of a pleasurable or frightening nature. Even if one should actually acquire access to astral, causal and celestial realms, the experience may be so enthralling that the ideal of final knowledge is forgotten.

Should soul abilities awaken and one find that unusual powers are at his disposal, it may be that these become so attractive that ego involvement with them leads the devotee from the enlightenment path. Let us remember that not all radiant beings in the subtle spheres are liberated. Many of them are somewhat Self-realized but also still somewhat deluded, that is, lacking in complete God-realization. The meditator's purpose, therefore, should be to pierce the veil of maya, primal substance, and experience pure consciousness. After being anchored in pure consciousness, one may then examine any and all possiblities, if there is purpose for so doing, without any possibility of self-deception or errors in judgment.

After Kriya pranayama, one should sit for a long time in the tranquil state generated by the practice. With attention flowing inward to the spiritual eye, one should look within and listen within, gently, observing any unfoldments. It is the calm state which is healing to the mind and body and which allows superconscious forces full play.

More advanced techniques will be given by the guru after the meditator has progressed in the practice of Kriya prana- yama. It is important that one fully explore all possibilities with preliminary techniques before progressing to others, as results from preliminary techniques make possible more ad- vanced practices. When one is proficient in practice, higher techniques will unfold from within his own consciousness, and these should be verified by the guru to insure that they are correct for the meditator.

A subtle but tempting attraction is for a meditator to falsely assume that he is receiving inner guidance from a spir- itual master on the astral or causal planes. This can occur, of course, but often what one assumes to be guidance from a master is but the inner wish-fulfillment of the meditator being expressed as subconsciously induced visions or "voices" which are prompted by impulses from deeper layers of the mind. Such inner plane communication should also be veri- fied, so that the meditator will clearly know whether or not he is receiving true assistance or is but involved with self- induced mental processes.

Kriya meditation techniques can be used by devotees in all walks of life. They are no longer only for monastics or the few among the many who have concluded their family and social responsibilities. The techniques should, however, be considered personal, and should not be taken lightly or loosely talked about with others. They are for dedicated persons who are fully committed on the path and who are willing to devote regularly scheduled times for their practice.

If you are a devotee on the path, if you are committed to the way of righteousness and to the ideal of unfolding your full soul potential in this life cycle, Kriya Yoga is for you. These practices need not interfere with the exercise of your traditional or preferred religious practices. A Christian can continue to honor the saints and emulate the life of Jesus. A Moslem can continue to worship as prescribed by his scripture. A Buddhist can follow the eightfold way and experience re- lease from the wheel of causation. A Hindu can worship ac- cording to his traditional ways. Persons who do not adhere to any traditional form of worship can honor the Great Life and realize the innate divine nature of the soul. There is no need to adapt different modes of worship if one is satisfied with his present way. There is no need to belong to any organized sect or movement, believing that by such involvement one is more likely to be "preferred in the eyes of God." It is useful, however, to honor all ways which others find helpful to them on the spiritual path, and to understand the underlying essence which lends vitality to them all.

When Mahavatar Babaji gave Lahiri Mahasaya permission to initiate others into Kriya Yoga practices, he instructed him to be sure that candidates for initiation were honest and truthful. This was the main consideration. It is important that one on the enlightenment path observe the rules of ideal behavior and be disciplined in all useful ways. New initiates were asked to make a symbolic donation to the guru's cause at the time of initiation and to thereafter assist him in his mission. A person who comes to a guru seeking initiation, is accepted and then later removes himself from association with the guru and his mission is obviously not dedicated on the path. He is merely self-centered, attempting to acquire for himself what he can and then go his way alone. This is not a noble characteristic for one on the discipleship path, and it will reflect as personal problems with the passage of time. A Kriya Yoga initiate should lead an exemplary life, study the prescribed scriptures and meditate deeply on a regular schedule. This is the way to success on the path.

The only way an initiate can fail to experience positive results is by being negligent in his practices. Do not be overly anxious to learn new and "more advanced" meditation procedures. Through devotion alone it is possible to experience Self-realization. Through prayer and contemplation it is possible to unfold. Through mantra meditation, and sound and light meditation, it is possible to advance on the path. The Kriya pranayama technique affords one the opportunity to quickly internalize attention and flow it to the source. Regularly practiced, it will result in the awakening of dormant forces, primal sound will be heard, and thought waves will be stilled, so that pure consciousness is naturally experienced.

Sri Yukteswar, in his book, *The Holy Science*, wrote of Kriya pranayama as follows:

> By culture of regulation of breath, as directed by the Spiritual Preceptor, the holy Word spontaneously appears and becomes audible. When this mantra appears, the breath becomes regulated and checks the decay of the material body.

Lahiri Mahasaya wrote commentaries on several scriptures, including the Yoga Sutras. A few of his comments follow:

> By sincere practice of Kriya, one attains the state wherein he realizes that all objects (of the senses) are nothing but the manifestations of the Self. He is no longer attached to them and attains inner wisdom and enlightenment.
>
> When the waves of the heart are transcended by sincere Kriya practice, the heart, being purified, becomes one with the Self. Thus the manifested world, the seeker's heart (essence) and the Self become one. The one Self is manifesting as three, and appears to be three so long as the ego remains.
>
> When memory is purified, then samadhi is experienced. When the feelings of memory are dissolved, the stable state of samadhi is realized. In that state of consciousness the manifested world appears as a mere shadow to the seeker as he realizes its essential nothingness.
>
> The inner realization of the Self is achieved only in the pure state of samadhi, which is absolutely free from thoughts.
>
> When the seeker attains inner wisdom, inner realization of the Self through samadhi, the attention is poised in inner wisdom and cannot go outward to form attachments.

When inward awareness is dissolved in the very Source, the true Self, then the perfect state is experienced, and the seeker attains eternal tranquility, the true liberation.

The righteous action, that is, Kriya practice without expectation of results, brings its effect, that is, attainment of liberation. While wrong action, Kriya practice with the expectation of results, brings inner enjoyment which, when it ceases, causes the seeker to turn back to his previous state, with its attachments.

All perceptions and visions are secondary. Whatever appears must disappear, hence, it cannot be permanent. Truth is eternal realization.

Removing ignorance by dissolving the ego is the only way to attain absolute knowledge. The aim of practicing Yoga is to dissolve the ego, removing the cause of ignorance.

When the seeker dissolves his mind in its Source he attains inner realization. When he attains the state wherein everything becomes one, the seeker is then attuned with eternal realization.

When the seeker is established in samadhi his practice becomes natural and spontaneous. In that state he does not have to practice with effort. Effort is shed, and without even practicing Kriya he enjoys the benefits.

Listening to the inner sound, the seeker actually sees gods, seers and sages of the past in the inner spiritual eye.

When the seeker transcends the awareness of meditation and is stable in inner awareness, which is similar to the void but full of bliss, he has reached the true state of samadhi.

There is absolutely one Self which is the ultimate existence. The seen is nothing but the reflection of the seer. The ultimate Self is the source of all.

When the yogi harmonizes his breath and experiences tranquility, his heart (essence) becomes calm by the practice of Kriya Pranayama. The influence of nature-born qualities are transcended. Then the seeker experiences the fullness of God, enters into oneness with the inner Self, and eventually with the ultimate Self. This is the highest state one can attain, which is eternal realization.

This approach is, then, the inner way to God-realization; it should be sincerely entered into by persons who are called to the enlightenment experience. Devoted attention to these basic practices will, in time, result in needed psychological changes, refinement and restructuring of the nervous system, and all else which is needed so that the light of the soul can shine fully through the body temple.

FOUR

Recommended Guidelines and Routines for Advanced Meditators

Paramahansa Yogananda used to say, "Make a daily appointment with God and keep that appointment. Everything else can wait, but your experience with God cannot wait!"

When you meditate, and how long and how often, will have to be decided by you, according to your aspiration and the circumstances with which you must coordinate your practice sessions. If you are single, or living with a husband or wife who shares your philosophical views, the scheduling of meditation will present no challenge. If domestic circumstances, for whatever reason, or occasional business activities must be considered, then do the best you can to arrange a time for meditation which will afford privacy and freedom for extended periods of meditation when inclined.

Shorter meditation sessions, commonly experienced by the average meditator, are useful for benefits mentioned in an earlier chapter. Advanced meditators, however, will want to provide for more time to deeply explore larger possibilities. Whereas the average meditator may practice once or twice a day for thirty minutes per session, the advanced meditator will want to allow an hour or more for each session, practicing for shorter periods when extended sessions are not convenient, or for centering and attunement purposes.

Prior to longer meditation sessions be sure to be relaxed, attend to bathroom needs, bathe if possible to cool the system and contribute to balancing of nerve forces, and approach the meditation nook with loving anticipation. Have a glass of water at hand for satisfying thirst if the meditation session will be longer than usual.

It would be helpful to have a meditation room set aside for this special purpose, and to have there a comfortable chair and a simple altar decorated to suit your devotional mood.

If you practice yogasanas prior to meditation, conclude with *mahamudra* and alternate nostril breathing, to enliven the system and balance prana flows.

Practicing Meditation

Begin with an invocation, opening your mind and heart to God. This can be either verbal or mental, to suit your mood. The words can be your own. A simple invocation is:

> Reverently I acknowledge the one Life, the infinite field of Consciousness. I acknowledge God, the omnipresent, omniscient, omnipotent. I acknowledge the Holy Spirit, the life of God. I acknowledge the order of the universe, the way of righteousness. I acknowledge the saints and sages of all enlightenment traditions. I acknowledge the divinity of every person. . . the divine essence in nature. . .and the divinity of myself. I acknowledge that as a specialized expression of pure consciousness I innately possess all of the attributes, qualities and capacities of God within me. I now contemplate the Supreme Self with a surrendered heart.

If you have been initiated into a guru line, acknowledge the gurus in that line and attune your mind and heart to them. If yours is the Christian tradition, acknowledge the living presence of the Christ of God, God actively expressing through all creation.

Sit quietly for a while, feeling close to God. Feel that God is all around you, through you, and in you. Remember that meditation is a natural, easy process and that an innate intelligence is working with you. Feel that you are sitting before, and surrounded by, an infinite ocean of consciousness which is your larger reality.

If you feel inclined to practice mantra meditation for a while, then do so with a surrendered attitude until you are calm and inwardly turned.

Then, practice Kriya pranayamas for the prescribed number of times, going more deeply within with each ascending flow of the current. After the last ascending flow, continue inward contemplation, leaving the current up, in the crown chakra, while being absorbed in the spiritual eye.

Remove your attention from the breathing process and flow inward, resting in the deep silence and dissolving in the tranquil calm of meditation. Meditation will continue spontaneously, without personal effort.

Sit for as long as comfortable in this manner. Thoughts will be minimal, perhaps dormant. Superconsciousness will be experienced easily.

If inner sound is heard, and if inner light is perceived, dissolve in sound and light, being drawn to the source of sound and light.

When Not to Practice
Kriya Pranayamas

If very ill and weak, do not practice dynamic Kriya pranayamas. Women, when pregnant, should not practice. It may also be well not to practice Kriya pranayamas during the few days when the monthly period is being experienced. Persons with serious heart problems should not practice dynamic Kriya pranayamas.

If, for any reason, Kriya pranayamas are not advised, then practice *mentally*, visualizing the current moving in the usual way, and then rest in the meditative silence. In this way the process will still balance internal systems and have a cleansing effect upon the subtle bodies and mental field.

Deeper Meditative
States and Samadhi

There are degrees of samadhi. Samadhi is experienced

when the waves of the mind are stilled and one remains alert. Sleep, unconsciousness, or the hypnotic state are not samadhi states. In early stages of samadhi it may appear to an observer that the meditator is in a trance state, but the meditator is not really unconscious. Instead, he is so inwardly absorbed that outer awareness is absent. Therefore, hypnotic states and various unconscious states should not be confused with samadhi. The former states do not result in illumination of consciousness, while samadhi does result in illumination and transformation of man's lower nature.

Initial samadhi states are referred to as "with difference," because the meditator is often conscious of being absorbed in the object of contemplation but still separate from God. The Sanskrit term for this state is *sabikalpa samadhi*. Samadhi "without difference" is *nirbikalpa samadhi*, during which the soul is fully conscious of its absorption in God. After extended periods of nirbikalpa samadhi experience one is fully aware of his relationship with God at all times, even when performing ordinary activities.

Repeated sabikalpa samadhi experiences result in memory of the experience when meditation is concluded, while steady nirbikalpa samadhi results in full God-consciousness, even after meditation.

During sabikalpa samadhi states one may, in the early stages, even doubt the experience and wonder if it is true or not. Deeper sabikalpa samadhi experiences result in complete absorption in the meditation object: light, sound, bliss, and so on, but this is not the highest state to which one should aspire.

After repeated nirbikalpa samadhi experiences one then lives in the *sahaja samadhi* state, the state of being spontaneously aware of the truth about the nature of Consciousness all of the time. One may then repeatedly experience meditation for the purpose of resting in pure consciousness alone, but will not feel diminished or apart from God even when not meditating. One who lives in the sahaja samadhi state sees the universe as a mere play of lights and shadows and knows the reality of Consciousness as both the unmanifest field and all that is manifesting. He knows the reality of Consciousness as formless and as formed. He does not consider the world of nature, then, as something from which to withdraw or something to fear. Whether water appears as vapor, liquid or ice, it is still water. Whether Consciousness is perceived as pure and devoid of qualities, as fine or subtle matter, or as gross matter, it is still Consciousness.

When the meditation session is concluded, sit for a while and rest in the calm state. Let this calmness permeate your mind and body. Feel yourself to be in harmony with your environment. If you feel led to do so, this can be the occasion for prayer on behalf of others or for more clearly examining your life and your priorities and relationships. Be happy, feel cheerful, and be settled in the awareness of God.

Longer Meditation
Sessions and Procedures

Now and then, once a week, twice a month or once a month, plan a longer meditation session, one which will extend to two or more hours. Begin as usual and meditate deeply after Kriya pranayama. When you feel yourself coming out of meditation you can pray for a while, or inwardly chant a mantra, or listen to your preferred mantra, until you are once again internalized.

Also, practice other meditation techniques as taught by your preceptor. Give more extended attention to the inner sound or the inner light, or both. If you have been taught how to focus at the spiritual eye, to see the inner light, do this. This technique can be learned from the guru or meditation teacher and involves a modified Kriya pranayama, along with special inward contemplation.

These periods of "personal retreat" can be extremely useful for deepening meditation and for centering. Especially if you are very busy and have had to miss some meditation sessions, an occasional longer session will be helpful in aiding you to be once again established in inner calm. During this time resolve to continue for the allotted time, even if meditation is not flowing smoothly. Do not put forth much effort, but remain seated and intent upon the purpose for which you have set aside the time. This will result in self-control and will improve your ability to be disciplined.

During long sessions, between periods of deep meditation it can be useful to read from a selected philosophical or devotional source for the purpose of motivation and inspiration. Then, read only a little, and contemplate what you have read, letting your thoughts take you into further contemplation and meditation.

Now and then, when and if possible, meditate with others who share your devotion to the path. This can reinforce you and be useful to all of the participants. But do not become dependent upon the company of others to the extent that you feel you cannot meditate without their presence. The inward journey can only be taken alone.

Meditating Through the "Path of God"

Either during your usual in-depth meditation session, or during longer ones, now and then practice the Kriya process of ascending the chakras, enlivening them as you proceed.

After prolonged meditation, when you feel the need for deepening your experience, use this process. Sitting upright with your back away from the chair (if you are sitting in a chair with a back on it), let your awareness be in the spinal pathway, "the path of God." Be aware of the brain, spiritual eye and length of the spinal pathway. Feel this pathway as though it were a hollow tube, up through which your feeling and awareness will ascend.

Looking into the spiritual eye, with your feeling centered at the base chakra, contract and relax the anal sphincter muscles a few times. Lifting up, holding the contraction, looking into the spiritual eye, mentally chant a very low-pitched mantra, "Om, Om, Om, Om, Om, Om, Om, Om, Om," etc. You may find it helpful, in the beginning, to chant this mantra audibly. Try to hit the pitch which results in vibrational activity at the chakra concentrated upon.

Use this mantra for the remaining chakras, in ascending

order. Starting with the base chakra, chant the mantra. Then locate the sacrum, the chakra in the small of the back, pull a Kriya current to that chakra, hold, and chant. Pause until breathing rhythm is restored.

Ascend to the lumbar chakra, pulling the Kriya current to that chakra, and chant the mantra. Continue through to each chakra, finishing with the crown chakra, then sit in deep meditation, letting the process be directed from within.

With prolonged practice of this technique, you may see the lights of the various chakras reflected in the spiritual eye, and you may hear inner sounds emanting from the chakras. At any rate the technique, when practiced regularly, will result in an enlivening of the chakras and a deepening of concentration during meditation.

Kundalini Awakening
and Inner Transformation

The word *kundalini* means "coiled, dormant potential." It refers to the potential soul force which is latent in man after the formation of the body. In unawakened people, some soul force is active, and this nourishes and maintains the body, but much soul force remains at rest. With spiritual awakening, however, this force begins to stir, resulting in enhanced vitality and an extension of creative ability. As it increases in activity it cleanses the pathways through which prana flows, unveils intuition, clears the intellectual faculty and improves powers of concentration.

Kundalini in man is the same as kundalini in nature. In nature, too, dormant potential rests. When it is attracted by the magnetic influence of God it results in evolution, and as it is currently being attracted more strongly it is resulting in accelerated planetary transformation and mass spiritual awakening among the planet's population.

The creative force of God in nature is the same as the creative force of the soul in man. It is one and the same force. Kundalini is awakened in man as a result of natural evolution, and as a result of aspiration, devotion, harmonious living, meditation, and the practice of such techniques as are part of the Kriya Yoga tradition.

It is not useful for one to attempt to awaken kundalini by forceful means. Kundalini awakens naturally when we think divine thoughts and yearn to know God. Then the magnetic attraction of God pulls it upward in a natural way, in accord with our capacity to respond to it. Therefore, we are not to attempt to push the current up; we are to *attract* it upwards, and Kriya pranayama will assist in this process.

There have been published accounts of personal experiences which have informed the reader of the "dangers" inherent in working with kundalini. In every one that I have read, the author revealed himself to be almost totally ignorant of kundalini processes. Most accounts which detail painful physical experiences and frightening psychological consequences are obvious testimonials to the emotional and psychological immaturity of the experimenting participant.

There can be physical changes, and certain psychological changes which can take place as the result of kundalini activity, but a person who is living a balanced life and who is engaged in devotional practices will not have any problems. The intelligence within, which directs all transformation processes, knows how to proceed in ways appropriate to personal needs.

Kundalini spontaneously awakens and moves when we are ready for such activity. It can also awaken because of strong devotion to God. It can be stirred into activity by the guru, either during initiation or when the moment is right for it to happen. One who is inwardly settled and who is attuned to a guru line will experience natural unfoldment and will be assisted from within by the supporting influence of God's grace.

Within the spinal pathway, at the subtle level, is the astral channel corresponding to the spinal cord. Prana circulates through it and in this manner the astral body is nourished. The practice of Kriya pranayama results in astral forces flowing along with the forces felt in the physical body and, in this way, the astral body is likewise purified and enlivened.

Even after transition from the physical body, Kriya prana-yama can be practiced while in the astral body. When, as the result of inner awakening, one becomes conscious of the astral spinal pathway, one becomes aware during meditation of astral spheres. In the same way, with continued awakening one becomes conscious of causal spheres and the spheres beyond the causal level.

It is not uncommon for a reasonably advanced meditator to at times experience real astral dreams and causal dreams, during which occasions they are actually communing with astral and causal inhabitants. Sometimes persons who are not yet consciously on the spiritual path commune with astral inhabitants.

Also, with purified awareness one may intuitively recognize the presence of astral beings or causal beings in his environment. Paramahansaji, and others I know, have told me of actually seeing saints in their subtle form, and of being able to see them at will by looking into the spiritual eye.

Once I was sitting near Paramahansaji when he was consoling two adults, children of one of his female disciples who had just recently made her transition. He looked into his spiritual eye for a moment, smiled sweetly, and said, "I just saw her. She is very happy where she is."

Through spiritual eye contact it is also possible to feel attunement with one's guru, or with anyone else one wants to commune with. This ability unfolds naturally, in time, and one need not be anxious for it to occur. When it does, it will be an easy thing to experience.

Balancing Meditation
Practice with Duties

It is extremely important that, while one is involved with an intentional meditation program, responsible attention is also given to living a practical, useful life and to attending to all duties with the right attitude. In this way balance is assured. To be focused in meditation but impractical and irresponsible in daily affairs is self-defeating and unbecoming to us as sincere devotees on the path.

We are, then, to the best of our ability live fully in this world and make a useful contribution to it. Let inner perceptions assist you in living an error-free life and let the radiance of Spirit shine through your every thought, word and deed. Paramahansaji used to say, "When you meditate you develop great powers of concentration which you can use to advantage in everyday living. And when you work with full attention you improve your powers of concentration, so that your meditations are more result-producing."

Paramahansaji himself was a perfect example of this teaching, and many of his spiritually advanced disciples also represented an ideal blend of spiritual realization and practical living. He acknowledged this and greatly admired it in others.

Others, too, who know of our interior life, will look to us to set an example for them. In the Bhagavad Gita (3:20—24) we read the following:

It was by selfless work that Janaka (a king who lived in India centuries ago) and others (like him) attained perfection. You should work also with the view of maintaining the world. Whatever a great man does, the same is done by others who look to him as an example. Whatever standard he sets, the world emulates. There is not, for Me, any (compulsive) work in the three worlds (physical, astral or causal) which has to be done, nor anything to be attained which has not been attained; yet I am engaged in action. For if I did not engage in ceaseless work, men on all levels of society might follow my example and the world would fall to ruin, and I would be responsible for the resulting discord and destruction.

It is not activity which is binding; it is attachment to the results of activity which binds us. It is not expressing through the senses which injures us, for the senses were made for such expression, but it is misuse of the senses which injures and binds.

Kriya meditation techniques, or ones very similar, have

been known and practiced by spiritual masters for thousands of years. Mahavatar Babaji has said that it was he who initiated many of the Yoga masters of renown, in centuries past, into Kriya meditation methods. Whenever such procedures fall into disuse, they are reintroduced when a new upward cycle occurs by the few souls on earth who are able to use them and benefit by their use. This is why they have been again made available to a God-seeking world in the present cycle.

Be intent on the spiritual path, finding fault with no one because of his station in life or chosen spiritual path. Avoid useless debate and shallow comparisons. The most important thing is for each of us to live, to the best of which we are capable, a life centered in God. Attention to the basic guidelines and deep, regular practice of meditation is all that is necessary for the fullness of God to be revealed to us.

FIVE

Surrendered Love
and Redeeming Grace

It is correct and proper for us to attend to needed disciplines—to study about the nature of consciousness, to meditate on a regular schedule, and to be faithful in our various spiritual practices. We do these things because they are helpful in assisting us to live ordered lives, to become knowledgeable, to cleanse mind and body, and to experience the pure nature of the soul and the reality of God.

Let it be clearly understood, however, that with all of our dedicated efforts, *something more* is required of us. This additional *something* is surrendered love in order to experience redeeming grace.

When our love for God is completely surrendered, God's love redeems us by grace. The love of God of which I speak is, except in rare instances, nothing like the highest love of which we are capable on the human level. When our love is pure, it is *divine love*, God's love expressing through us. The love of God is the attracting force which unveils the soul and replaces darkness with light. This is why we can say that surrendered love results in our experiencing redeeming grace.

Grace is the activity of the Holy Spirit, transforming and enlightening us. It cannot be earned. It is not the effect of any cause. The only thing we can do is prepare ourselves to experience it and be open to that experience. When the moment is right for us to be influenced by it fully, it will be experienced without fail. When grace is present in our lives our soul freedom is assured, because it will, in time, make all necessary adjustments, within and without, to ensure the completion of its purposes. The activity of grace results in the unfoldment in us of all of the divine qualities, so that the virtues which we once vainly attempted to actualize blossom naturally in us. This is not to say that our personal efforts are not useful—they are, as preparation for what is to come when grace begins to work through us.

When I met Paramahansaji he said, "When you came to me, God took fifty per cent of your karma, guru's grace assumes twenty-five per cent, and you have the rest to work out yourself." What he meant was that when one commits himself to the enlightenment path he avoids all of the future problems he might have experienced had he not repented, had he not turned to the source. God's grace, through the guru, enlivens us and counsels us so that we can unfold quickly on the path. But it is our personal responsibility to order our lives, live in harmony with natural laws, improve our understanding, and practice spiritual disciplines for the purpose of opening ourselves to the awareness of the reality of God.

Grace is Present
at All Times

The attracting force of God is ever involved with creation. It is responsible for evolution, for transformation and ordered unfoldment in nature and in man. It works through us even when we are not aware of its presence. It directs us along the upward way when we are not even aware of such a way, and it results in our spiritual awakening and our turning to God. Finally, when we are ready to experience accelerated unfoldment, its influence is more dynamic, more obvious, and it causes us to experience higher states of consciousness.

It sometimes happens that persons who are not intentionally on the enlightenment path experience breakthroughs which change them forever. It also happens that persons, after months or years of study and meditation, suddenly experience uplift and degrees of illumination of consciousness.

Grace does this, and since it is directed by the intelligence of God it always works perfectly in our lives.

I speak from experience, because I have been aware of a guiding influence in my life since childhood, and I have seen evidence of a regulating intelligence in my personal affairs. It has been as though a benevolent "presence" was looking after the things I did not know how to attend to, that its plan and purpose were assured of being fulfilled, even during those times when the plan and purpose were not completely clear to me, or when I was aware of the plan but not how to fulfill it.

As we continue on the enlightenment path we experience initiation after initiation, one "new beginning" after another. These are states of soul unfoldment during which, if we are patient and attentive enough, we learn to function at ever-new levels of conscious understanding. We awaken from the sense of mortality to the realization of immortality, and the enlightenment process becomes more clear with each passing day.

Let us hear from a few kindred souls who, like ourselves, have been open to the transforming influence of grace. The Buddha, speaking of illumination, said that it "will cause a man to become"

> . . .beloved, popular, respected among his fellows, victorious over discontent and lust; will bestow upon him the ecstasy of contemplation; will enable him to reach with his body, and remain in, those stages of deliverance which are incorporeal and pass beyond phenomena; cause him to become an inheritor of the highest heavens; make him becoming one to become multiple, being multiple to become one; will endow him with clear and heavenly ear, surpassing that of men; enable him to comprehend by his own heart the hearts of other beings and of other men, to understand all minds, the passionate, the calm, the angry, the peaceable, the deluded, the wise, the concentrated, the sublime, the mean, the steadfast, the wavering, the free and the enslaved; give him power to call to

mind his various temporary states in days gone by;
such as one birth, two births, three, four, five, ten,
twenty, thirty, forty, fifty, a hundred, a thousand or
a hundred thousand births: his births in many an eon
of renovation; in many an eon of both destruction
and renovation; to call to mind his temporary states
in days gone by in all their modes and in all their details; to see with pure and heavenly vision surpassing
that of men, beings as they pass from one state of
existence and take form in others; beings base or noble,
goodlooking or ill-favored, happy or miserable: to
know and realize emancipation of heart and emancipation of mind.

With illumination of consciousness, soul capacities are expressed naturally, and these are to be used wisely and appropriately. But regardless of the extent to which these abilities
can be demonstrated, we must be ever reminded that to be
open to God's will, through grace, is the most important condition of all. In The First Epistle of Paul the Apostle to the
Corinthians (13: 1—13) we read:

Though I speak with the tongues of men and of
angels, but have not love, I have become as sounding
brass or a clanging cymbal. And though I have the gift
of prophecy, and understand all mysteries and all
knowledge, and though I have all faith, so that I could
remove mountains, but have not love, I am nothing.
And though I bestow all my goods to feed the poor,
and though I give my body to be burned, but have
not love, it profits me nothing. Love suffers long and
is kind, love does not envy; love does not parade itself,
is not puffed up (arrogant); does not behave rudely,
does not seek its own, is not provoked, thinks no evil;
does not rejoice in iniquity, but rejoices in the truth;
bears all things, believes all things, hopes all things,
endures all things. Love never fails. But whether there
are prophecies, they will fail; whether there is knowl-

edge, it will vanish away. For we know in part and we prophecy in part. But when that which is perfect has come, then that which is in part will be done away. When I was a child I spoke as a child; but when I became a man, I put away childish things. For now we see in a mirror, dimly, but then face to face. Now I know in part, but then I shall know just as I also am known. And now abide faith, hope, love, these three; but the greatest of these is love.

Plotinus, a Greek philosopher who lived during the second century A.D., wrote the following in a letter to a friend:

You ask, how can we know the Infinite? I answer, not by reason. It is the office of reason to distinguish and define. The Infinite, therefore, cannot be ranked among its objects. You can only apprehend the Infinite by a faculty superior to reason, by entering into a state in which you are your finite self no longer—in which the divine essence is communicated to you. This is ecstasy. It is the liberation of your mind from its finite consciousness. Like can only apprehend like; when you thus cease to be finite you become one with the Infinite. In the reduction of your soul to its simplest self, its divine essence, you realize this union—this identity.

But this sublime condition is not of permanent duration. It is only now and then that we can enjoy this elevation (mercifully made possible for us) above the limits of the body and the world. . . . All that tends to purify and elevate the mind, will assist you in this attainment, and will facilitate the approach and recurrence of these happy intervals. There are, then, different roads by which this end may be reached. The love of beauty which exalts the poet; that devotion to the One and that ascent of science which makes the ambition of the philosopher; and that love and those prayers by which some devout and ardent soul tends in its moral purity towards perfection. These are the great highways conducting to that height above the actual and the particular, where we stand in the immediate presence of the Infinite, who shines out as from the deeps of the soul.

Dante, the thirteenth century Italian poet, shared, in his literary works, his experiences. In his early years his intense desire to know about the universe caused him to study "theology, astrology, arithmetic and geometry, and history." In one of his writings, he refers to the guiding intelligence responsible for his illumination experiences as "Beatrice":

> Beatrice was standing with her eyes wholly fixed on the eternal wheels (of causation?), and on her I fixed my eyes from there above removed. Looking at her, I inwardly became such as Glaucus (the steersman of the ship Argo who was changed into a god) became on tasting of the herb which made him consort in the sea of the other gods. Transhumanizing cannot be signified in words; therefore, let the example suffice for whom grace reserves experience. O love that governest the heavens, thou knowest, who with thy light didst lift me.

St. John of the Cross (Juan Yepes) was a Carmelite monk in Spain five hundred years ago. In one of his writings this saintly person shared of his experiences:

> Though it be true, as I have said, that God is always in every soul, bestowing upon it and preserving it, by His presence, its natural being, yet for all this He does not always communicate the supernatural life. For this is given only by love and grace, to which all souls do not attain, and those who do, do not in the same degree, for some rise to higher degrees of love than others. That soul, therefore, has greater communion with God which is most advanced in love—that is,

whose will is most conformable to the will of God. And that soul which has reached perfect conformity and resemblance is perfectly united with, and supernaturally transformed in God. For which cause, therefore, as I have already explained, the more the soul cleaves to created things, relying on its own strength, by habit and inclination, the less it is disposed for this union, because it does not completely resign itself into the hands of God, that He may transform it supernaturally.

Surrendered love which prepares one for the influence of redeeming grace is not a casual devotional approach. It is a matter of loving God with all our heart, mind and soul, to the extent that our yearning to experience reality is all-consuming. It is the desire to know the truth while, at the same time, being surrendered to God's will. In this way our love is not frantic and emotional; it is intense, yet trusting.

When we love in this way we dutifully engage in all needed practices in preparation for what is surely to unfold. An examination of the lives of those who have experienced illumination of consciousness reveals an earnest desire to realize the soul's full potential, although individual approaches may vary. A superficial interest in spiritual matters does not suffice; such a life has no focus, because the heart's desire has not been defined. What is required is discipleship, commitment to the ideal, and this commitment is the central factor around which everything else in our lives revolves.

The *way* is known, because it has been experienced by others who have shared their knowledge of it. The way is open to all, and accessible to all. Each person unfolds according to personal destiny, and the final result is the same. Although we cannot see them with ordinary sight, all around us are shining beings who share with us their radiance and their benevolence. We do not tread the path alone. Grace, through personal and impersonal manifestations, is ever assisting us in the direction of final knowledge.

When you are very quiet, when neither memories nor

thoughts of present matters float in your mind and consciousness, you inwardly know the reality of your being. You know
you are pure, clear, unborn and undying—forever the same as
pure consciousness. This is your real nature. It cannot be improved upon and it cannot be changed in any way.

The experience of cosmic consciousness, oneness with the
cosmos, does not grant knowledge of all relative occurrences,
but it does result in the realization of harmony with all life.
From this level of awareness, we are then able to move through
space and time with inward assurance, always appropriate
and in the flow of grace. It is then natural to love God and all
expressions of God.

Cosmic consciousness will surely be increasingly experienced by every person in our awakening era. This is the vision
of the seers of the ages and the testimony of increasing numbers of men and women around the world. Jesus referred to
cosmic consciousness as the experience of "the kingdom of
heaven"; other seers have referred to it in various ways. It is
that, once we have learned of it, for which we will do anything in order to allow it to unfold in our consciousness.

Until it is our permanent realization, we have the guidelines of the masters before us to consider and to follow. We
are to live a decent, well-ordered life. We are to study, pray,
and meditate. We are to serve others and our world. We are to
desire the conscious awareness of the reality of God, every
waking moment, until we are so attuned to the magnetic love
of God that grace redeems us, lifting us from the darkness of
unknowingness to the light of knowledge.

This is the way for everyone. It is the way for you, it is
the way for others, it is the way for me. When all else has
been said and done, surrendered love and redeeming grace
completes the process.

BIBLIOGRAPHY

Ballentine, Rudolph, M.D. *Diet & Nutrition.* Honesdale, Pa.: Himalayan International Institute, 1978.

Bartlett, John. *Familiar Quotations.* Boston/Toronto: Little, Brown & Co., 1980.

Bhattacharya, Jogesh Chandra. *Yogiraj Shri Shri Lahiri Mahasaya.* Howrah, India: Srigurudham (Yogoda Satsanga), 1969.

Bucke, Richard Maurice, M.D. *Cosmic Consciousness.* New York: E.P. Dutton Co., 1969.

Caraka Samhita. Varanasi, India: Chowkhamba Sanskrit Series Office, 1983.

Chopra, Deepak, M.D. *Total Health: The Rediscovery of Ayurveda.* Cassette tape album. Fairfield, Ia.: Maharishi Ayurveda Products Intl., Inc., 1986.

Dasgupta, Salendra Bejoy. *Kriya Yoga and Swami Sriyukteswar.* Calcutta: S.B. Das Gupta, 1979.

Dash, Vaidya Bhagwan. *Fundamentals of Ayurvedic Medicine.* New Delhi: Bansal & Co., 1982.

Electricity in Foods: "Celestial Fire Stepped Down in Fruits." Edited by Carque Natural Brands Research Fndn. *Inner Culture,* Vol. XII, No. 9. Los Angeles: Self-Realization Fellowship.

Eliade, Mircea. *Yoga, Immortality and Freedom.* New York: Princeton Univ. Press, 1973.

Hatha Yoga Pradipika. New Delhi: Oriental Books Reprint Corp.

Katumbiah, P., M.D. *Ancient Indian Medicine.* Madras: Orient Longmans, 1962.

Lad, Vasant. *Ayurveda: The Science of Self-Healing.* Santa Fe: Lotus Press, 1986.

_____ and Frawley, David. *The Yoga of Herbs.* Santa Fe: Lotus Press, 1986.

Ott, John N. *Light, Radiation, and You.* Greenwich, Conn.: Devin-Adair Pub., 1982.

Radhakrishnan, S.   *The Principal Upanishads.* London/New York: George Allen & Unwin, Ltd., and New York Humanities Press, Inc., 1953.

Rama, Swami. *Perennial Philosophy of the Bhagavad Gita.* Honesdale, Pa.: Himalayan International Institute, 1985.

Schumann, Walter. *Gemstones of the World.* New York: Sterling Pub. Co., Inc., 1977.

Sushruta Samhita. Translated from the Sanskrit by Kaviraj Nunjalal. Varanasi, India: Chowkhamba Sanskrit Series Office, 1981.

Thakkur, Chandrashekhar, G. *Introduction to Ayurveda.* New York: ASI Pub., Inc., 1974.

Treadway, Scott, and Linda Treadway. *Ayurveda and Immortality.* Berkeley: Celestial Arts, 1986.

Walford, Roy L., M.D. *Maximum Life Span.* New York/London: W.W. Norton & Co., 1983.

Yogananda, Paramahansa. *Autobiography of a Yogi.* Los Angeles: Self-Realization Fellowship, 1946.

Yukteswar, Swami Sri. *The Holy Science.* Los Angeles: Self-Realization Fellowship, 1949.

GLOSSARY

Whenever a word's meaning is not understood, comprehension of the theme will be incomplete. Refer to this section often, until words and meanings are clear in mind. Many of the words here used are Sanskrit, which means "polished" or "perfected." It will not be necessary for the average reader to become a Sanskrit scholar, but it will be helpful to understand the meanings of the words.

Absolute. The non-dual field of Consciousness. The Transcendental Field. The "void" of the Buddhist, which is really the absence of modification, but which contains the essence of all possibilities.

Actualize. To "make real" or to bring into manifestation. Capacities are actualized when used and demonstrated. Goals are actualized when they become manifest.

Advaita. Non-duality; the teaching that everything in the manifest realms is an expression of one thing, Consciousness.

Ahamkara. The ego, or personal sense of being separate from God. Because of this initial error in perception the soul erroneously feels itself to be independent of that which is its larger reality.

Akasa. Often spelled "akasha"; the first of five material elements making up the field of manifest nature. Translated into English as "ether," or fine substance. The remaining four elements are air, fire, water, and earth (gross particles).

Ananda. Literally, bliss. Often used as part of a monastic name by yogis. Example: Yogananda, "bliss through Yoga, or divine union."

Asana. Pose or posture. Yogasanas are the various poses assumed in practicing Hatha Yoga. Sitting poses are used for meditation. The ideal pose for meditation is upright and steady, so the body is comfortable and not inclined to waver while one is absorbed in quiet contemplation.

Ashram. A quiet secluded place for study and spiritual practice. Ideally, an ashram should provide an environment in which residents can live close to nature and where outside distractions are not possible. Only elevating influences should prevail, so that all of the virtues are naturally encouraged to unfold.

Atma. The divine Self of every person. It is this divine Self which is to be consciously realized by the seeker on the spiritual path. When realization is experienced, one knows the true Self to be cosmic, even while assuming various viewpoints, known as souls.

Avadhut. A supremely enlightened person who functions through mind and body while simultaneously being aware of omnipresence. In his later years, after experiencing transcendental states of consciousness, Paramahansa Yogananda told close disciples, "From now on I will appear to be as before, I will relate to you through this personality, but this personality is not the real me."

Avatar. The descent of divine power into human form. A full incarnation of God. Usually such manifestations are for the purpose of infusing planetary consciousness with divine influence. Sometimes avatars play a dramatic role; at other times they remain unknown to those around them. Their redemptive work is purely in line with God's will. Some work with the public, others remain in seclusion. It is entirely a matter of God's will.

Avidya. The word means "not knowledge," in contrast to the word *vidya*, which means full knowledge of Consciousness.

Ayurveda. Science of life. Said to have its basis in life itself, therefore without beginning. According to mythology, the science of Ayurveda passed from the gods to man. Chinese medicine is also believed to have been passed down from a previous Golden Age, and there is a similarity between Ayurvedic and Chinese medical procedures. Both include a total examination of the patient—pulse, temperature, skin condition, condition of the eyes, psychological makeup, and other factors, when making a diagnosis. Ayurveda uses diet, herbs, water therapy, massage, attitude training, detoxification procedures, and other procedures to encourage restoration of the body to a condition of balance. The *Charaka Samhita*, a famous Indian medical text, was preserved for generations by oral tradition before being written down. Using Sanskrit, practitioners of Ayurveda would memorize key phrases and in this way retain the knowledge of their science, as well as pass it on to qualified successors. First put into writing during the first century A.D., the *Charaka Samhita* lists over five hundred herbs and their medicinal uses. Knowledge of Ayurvedic procedures passed from India to Mediterranean countries and finally to the West. During the many years of British rule, state patronage resulted in a decline of Ayurvedic practice in India and Western medicine became dominant. Now, however, there are once again several schools of Ayurveda in India, and scientific research is being used to prove the usefulness of many of the procedures.

Bhagavad Gita. "God's glorious celestial song." A much-loved scripture in which Krishna, a divine incarnation, explains to Arjuna, his disciple, the philosophy of "the eternal way of righteousness" and the way to freedom in God. The reverent reading of the *Gita* cannot fail to result in a profound impact upon the mind and consciousness of the reader.

Bhagavan. Lord. Literally, one endowed with the six attributes: infinite spiritual power, righteousness, glory, splendor, knowledge, and renunciation.

Bhakti. Intense devotional love for God which results in understanding and respect for all of creation. A common teaching of yogis is that love for God leads to knowledge, and knowledge of God results in love.

Brahma. The initial expanding and projecting aspect of the Godhead which results in creation.

Brahmacharya. Spiritual discipline which enables one to acquire control over vital forces and mental and emotional tendencies.

Brahmaloka. The abode of God, corresponding to the highest sphere or realm this side of the Transcendental Field. According to Vedic teachings, only the Transcendental Field is pure, without characteristics of any kind, and everything this side of it is endowed with characteristics and influences, including the field of God.

Brahman. The Supreme Reality, the Absolute.

Brahma Sutras. Also known as the *Vedanta Sutras*. Revelations and philosophical speculations of the seers of Vedic times. Sutras, "threads," are concise statements designed to share understanding and to be contemplated by the student so that the student comes to experience his own revelation about the theme mentioned. Massive commentaries have been written on various sutras which have been compiled.

Buddha. A man who lived in northern India about 500 B.C.

Of royal birth, as a young man he became troubled when he saw the sufferings of the average person in society. Leaving home after marrying and fathering a son, he practiced extreme yogic procedures. Later he adopted the "middle way," the way of controlled moderation. He attained illumination and, thus, his name, "The Enlightened One," the Buddha. After his illumination he walked up and down the Ganges Valley for almost fifty years, preaching freely to all and forming a society of renunciate monks. He taught love, non-hatred, dedication to truth, the elimination of wishful thinking, and non-dependence on anything external, including religious ceremony. Illumination, as Buddhists teach, is not a state of consciousness, but the realization of the True Self which is common to us all.

Buddhi. The faculty of discernment possessed by man; the intellectual capacity. When, through discernment, one comprehends the totality of Consciousness, he is a buddha, an enlightened being. All beings possess a buddha nature because all beings are specialized expressions of Supreme Consciousness. When one knows his nature, instead of *about* his nature, he is spiritually free.

Capacity. The power or ability to receive or contain. The power or ability to do, to exercise abilities.

Chakra. A distribution center in the body through which prana flows. The main chakras, or "wheels," are located as follows: crown chakra, upper brain; spiritual eye, between the eyebrows, and the positive pole of the *medulla oblongata*; cervical chakra, in the spinal pathway opposite the throat; dorsal chakra, between the shoulder blades; lumbar chakra, middle of the back; sacral chakra, small of the back; and coccygeal chakra, the lower extremity of the spinal column. Prana flows into the body through the *medulla*, to the brain, and then down the spinal pathway to nourish the body and direct internal processes. The

spiritual eye center is used as a point of focus during yogic
meditation.

Downflowing prana changes in frequency as it flows
through the chakras in order to perform various functions.
The ether element is predominant at the throat chakra.
It is here that yogis concentrate when they desire to nourish the body without taking food. In descending order, the
air element is predominant at the dorsal chakra, fire at the
lumbar chakra, water at the sacral chakra, and earth at the
coccygeal chakra. It is possible to stimulate the activity of
prana at the different chakras by reciting certain mantras.

Chiropractic. Manipulation of the vertebral column for the
purpose of relieving nerve flow disturbances. B.J. Palmer,
"father of Chiropractic," taught, "We work with the subtle substance of the soul. We release the imprisoned impulse, the tiny rivulet of force, that flows over the nerves
to cells and stirs them into life. We deal with the majestic
power that transforms common foods into living, loving,
thinking clay; that robes the earth with beauty and hues
and scents the flowers with the glory of the air."

Chiti. Supreme Consciousness in its aspect as dynamic creative
power.

Chitta. The storehouse of memory, making possible the process of thinking.

Christ. The Christ of God is that aspect of the Godhead which
is actively involved with the world process. The Christ of
God is often referred to as the "only begotten of the Father" or the first emanation from the Godhead. It is the
Lord, or ruler of all that takes place in nature. The Jesus
of history was an avatar who fully allowed the Christ of
God to express in His life. He said, "I of myself can do
nothing; the Father within, he doeth the works."

Consciousness. Consciousness is of two kinds. One, there is the consciousness (awareness) of something. Two, there is the entity of consciousness itself, knowing itself as such, without any object or mirror for itself to be perceived in. The second kind is often referred to as pure consciousness. It is also the ground out of which all forms emerge.

Darshan. The blessing one receives as a result of looking upon a saint. To see a saint is to see divine qualities expressed through another, and to experience divine consciousness.

Deva. A "shining one" or god. Gods and goddesses (devis) are souls which dwell in subtle celestial realms.

Dharma. The upholding influence in nature which supports creation and maintains the evolutionary process. The term also refers to evolutionary order, the way of righteousness. The ideal way to live is to live in harmony with the way of righteousness. In this way we cooperate with the world process and we are upheld by it.

Dhatu. Literally, the ' supporting tissues" of the body. These are fluid essence (plasma), blood, muscle, fat, bone, marrow, and reproductive essence.

Diksha. Yogic initiation, during which instruction is given in meditation procedure and the guru transmits his spiritual force to the disciple. Instruction may vary, depending upon the teaching tradition represented by the guru, and by what the disciple needs to help him be successful on the path. Sometimes a mantra is given, sometimes pranayama is taught, and sometimes the disciple is instructed to look within and contemplate the true nature.

Dosha. In the Ayurvedic approach to wellness, major consideration is given to balancing the three governing principles, the doshas. These are the influences of Air, Fire and Water which determine body constitution and function.

God. The Supreme Being. The stable aspect of God is Pure Consciousness. When we think of God we usually conceptualize the Godhead, with attributes and capacities. Men have given the Godhead many names; so long as one turns to God, regardless of the name used, one is lifted Godward.

Guna. The three gunas are the characteristics and qualities of all nature. Sattwa guna is the force of equilibrium in nature which translates itself into the qualities of good, purity, harmony, balance, happiness, sympathy, light, virtue and knowledge. Rajas guna is the force of energy and motion in nature which translates itself into the qualities of passion, action, struggle, effort, and desire. Tamas guna is the force of inertia and inconscience in nature which translates itself into the qualities of inaction, ignorance, incapacity, darkness and obscurity. Sattwa guna brings illumination to the mind and impels one in the direction of right action and harmony. Rajas guna encourages one to strive, to resist, to attempt to dominate one's environment, to assert will, to fight, to create, to conquer, and to aspire. Tamas guna binds a person through negligence, error and inaction.

The *Gita* teaches that one should cultivate Sattwa guna to avoid being enslaved by Rajas guna or Tamas guna; one should then rise above the influence of even Sattwa guna by experiencing transcendental awareness.

Guru. Literally, the light that dispels darkness. The guru is considered to be God expressing in human form in order to assist disciples who seek liberation of consciousness. For a disciple to be successful in his efforts on the spiritual path he must please his guru; that is, he must abide by the guru's teachings. If the disciple resists the guru's teachings, if he is immature and self-willed, he is not open to higher instruction, nor to the possibility of transcending ego-consciousness. The guru's function is to show the disciple the way to freedom in God. For this to be possible, the disciple must be willing to rid himself of all that is contrary to Self-realization. Guruseva, service to the guru, is to be considered as service to God. By becoming attuned to the guru's consciousness the disciple experiences attunement to God. By understanding the true nature of the guru, the disciple understands the true nature of God.

Hinduism. The name given by foreign invaders to the religious practices of the people of India. The Sindhu river, flowing into the Arabian Sea, forms part of the western boundary of India. It was known by the ancient Persians as the "Hindu" river. The Greeks borrowed the name, changing it into "Indos," later converted into English as "Indus." The Greeks called the country east of "Indos" by the name of India. Its inhabitants became known as Hindus, and their religion as "Hinduism." Even today, many people in India refer to themselves as Hindus. Those who are more precise refer to their religious philosophy and practice as Sanatana Dharma, "the eternal way of righteousness."

Holy Spirit. The life of God expressed throughout the universe. It is the Holy Spirit aspect of God which enlivens the world, and man.

Homeopathy. A system of medicine that stimulates the individual to recuperate and cure himself. Homeopathic remedies are medicinal preparations which facilitate the process of self-cure and enable the organism to heal itself by following the laws of nature. The principles of Homeopathy date back to India's Ayurvedic system and to the teachings of Hippocrates of ancient Greece. Samuel Hahnemann, German chemist and physician, began to verify and codify these concepts in the eighteenth century. He coined the name Homeopathy.

Imagination. The ability to visualize, or picture in the mind's eye, new and novel possibilities. Imagination differs from daydreaming or wishful thinking only in degree; controlled imagination allows one to clearly define the mental picture.

Islam. Mohammed is the inspired prophet of Islam, which acknowledges the One God and respects all religious endeavors which have a Bible, a book of revealed truth. A true Islamite is dedicated to God and chooses to surrender his life to God.

Isvara. The personal aspect of God which governs and regulates creation. This aspect of God is referred to as the Lord, the ruling influence in nature.

Japa. The repetition of any of the names of God, for the purpose of concentration and meditation. A japmala is a string of beads used to assist in concentration and to count the repetitions.

Jaya. Victory. Often spelled "ji." "Ji Guru!" means "Victory to the guru!"

Jivanmukta. A liberated soul which is still embodied. Traces of karma may yet remain, but the soul is inwardly free and will not have to be reincarnated except it be God's will. Future actions of a jivanmukta are determined, not by karmic compulsion, but by God's will.

Jnana. Knowledge of God.

Judaism. The religious system of the Jewish people.

Kalpa. A cycle of time. Planet Earth experiences periodic changes, resulting in varied conditions for man. One Grand Cycle is about 24,000 years in duration, with sub-cycles of 4,800 years, 3,600 years, 2,400 years, and 1,200 years. The longest of the sub-cycles is an era of enlightenment, when civilizations flourish and order and harmony are experienced by the people. When order begins to break down, the 3,600-year cycle is experienced, during which time the people's capacity to discern the subtle side of life diminishes. This is followed by the 2,400-year descending phase, and finally the 1,200-year phase. After 1,200 years of Dark Age conditions, then another 1,200-year ascending Dark Age phase unfolds, followed by the other eras in reverse order. The last Dark Age, contrary to some popular teachings, ended about A.D. 1700, and the world is now pulling free of that Age's influences. This is why we are now witnessing rapid spiritual awakening, while humanity longs for the ideal world condition which it knows will unfold. The sub-cycles are referred to as yugas, or ages.

Karma. The law of causation; an action resulting in a reaction. The thoughts we think, the actions we perform, determine our day-to-day experiences. Also, the accumulated mental and emotional conflicts contribute to mental states and states of consciousness. The more God-conscious we are, the less prior causes influence present behavior and circumstances. Traumatic experience can, in some instances, result in impressions being made in the brain and cells of the body, interfering with function. In this way some karmic effects can be transmitted to children; that is, children can inherit the characteristics of the parents. The ideal, for one on the spiritual path, is to be free from karmic influences, and to live spontaneously from the awareness of being. Then whatever is done is done in the most appropriate manner to meet existing needs, and such actions do not bind one to future effects. They are actionless-actions.

Kaya-kalpa. A process undergone by some yogis to reverse the ravages of time on their bodies. A rejuvenation process which involves internal cleansing, the use of certain herbs, prolonged rest, and much meditation. To ensure seclusion, the yogi usually remains in a cave or a dwelling far removed from society. One yogi who underwent the kaya-kalpa process three times finally made his transition when he was over one hundred and eighty years of age. The first time he experienced the process, emerging after several months in seclusion, he appeared to be at least twenty years younger than when he began; his hair had returned to its natural color and he had grown a third set of teeth. It is rumored that there are yogis in the Himalayas who use this process to retain the body for hundreds of years. Chinese folklore also contains stories of the mortal-immortals who have learned to remain forever youthful.

Kundalini. Dormant static force resting in nature and in the body of man. When it awakens in nature, life forms begin on the planet. When it awakens in man, soul qualities begin to unfold. In the average person this force is mostly dormant and the person assumes himself to be a physical body. When kundalini awakens and begins to ascend the path of the chakras, then intellectual capacities are unveiled, intuition awakens, and creativity unfolds.

Lahiri Mahasaya. Disciple of Mahavatar Babaji who was chosen to introduce the practice of Kriya Yoga into the mainstream of society. Born September 30, 1828 in Bengal, India, he entered mahasamadhi at Benares on September 26, 1895.

Love. The attracting influence of God is the supreme expression of love, for it draws souls back to a conscious relationship with the Source. Human beings speak of love of country, love of mankind, love for another, and love as affection, or caring but unemotional friendship. All expressions of love are aspects of the soul's love of God. Love is purifying because it calls forth our best qualities, and demands of us surrender to the highest and best in any relationship.

Mahasamadhi. Conscious transition from the body. *Maha* means "great"; mahasamadhi, then, means the "great" or final samadhi. The term is also used to refer to a shrine which may be erected over the tomb of an enlightened yogi.

Mahavatar Babaji. Mortal-immortal master who yet lives in seclusion and guides the Kriya Yoga work through the guru line.

Mantra. A meditation mantra serves as an attractive focus of attention, so that attention can be led beyond mental processes to the experience of transcendence. Mantras may also be used to influence forces in nature, and to control and regulate such forces.

Maya. The fabric or "stuff" of which nature is formed. The components of maya are light particles, space, time, and the creative force from which they unfold. One characteristic of maya is that it is form-producing, as a mother is form-producing. Another characteristic is that it is truth-veiling; when a soul is identified too strongly with nature it experiences a diminishing of its intuitive and intellectual capacities, and becomes deluded. Maya is illusory, but it is not "illusion." Man, blinded by overidentification with matter, experiences errors in perception and knows but a portion of the allness of Consciousness.

Meditation. The easy process of relaxing the body and allowing the mental field to become clear. It has nothing in common with mental manipulation or hypnotic practices. Meditation is not a passive experience; it is a conscious, creative process. Patanjali's *Yoga Sutras* remains the most reliable guidebook to meditation practice. His explanation is sometimes referred to as "eight-limbed," because eight stages are explained. These are: Yama, the restraints; Niyama, the observances; Asana, correct meditation posture; Pranayama, regulation of vital forces in the body; Pratyahara, inward turning; Dharana, concentration; Dhyana, contemplation; Samadhi, clear awareness, the peak experience.

Moksha. Liberation of consciousness, resulting in knowledge and freedom from delusion.

Mudra. A symbolic pose or gesture. Also, a yogic procedure used to stimulate vital forces in the body and to afford the yogi conscious control over involuntary processes.

Nada. Different sounds heard within during meditation. These are variations of OM, the primal sound.

Nadi. A channel through which prana flows in the subtle body. For instance, ida is the left channel along the spinal pathway through which the "moon" current flows. Pingala is the right channel through which the "sun" current flows. During the course of a given day the force of flow through these channels will change, resulting in mood shifts and adjustments in states of consciousness. When these currents are in a condition of equilibrium, then prana flows with greater force in the sushumna, the central channel in the spinal pathway, and the mind is calm, allowing for introspection and successful meditation.

Nadi-Shuddi. The purification of the nadis, and the nervous system, as a result of active-flowing prana being encouraged through the practice of certain pranayamas and mudras. This also occurs naturally when kundalini is awakened.

Nirguna-Brahma. Supreme Consciousness without attributes or qualities. Saguna-Brahma refers to Consciousness with attributes and qualities.

OM. The primal sound current from which all other manifestations in nature are evolved. OM is also considered the highest, or most pure, mantra to be contemplated during meditation.

Omnipotence Unrestricted power, the power of God.

Omnipresence. Present everywhere simultaneously.

Omniscience. Being conscious everywhere.

Paramahansa. The highest spiritual reference given to a Self-realized yogi. A paramahansa is one who can live in the world and be untouched by any of the qualities of the world.

Paramahansa Yogananda. Chief disciple of Sri Yukteswar who brought the science of Kriya Yoga to the West. Born in India, 1893, entered mahasamadhi in Los Angeles, California, on March 7, 1952.

Paramukta. Enlightenment with no trace of karmic involvement. Jivanmukta is enlightenment with seeds of karma remaining. Paramukta is final liberation of consciousness.

Prakriti. Nature, consisting of elements and qualities. Purusha is the divine force which enlivens Prakriti.

Prana. Life force which permeates the universe. Pranas are frequencies of the creative current flowing from the Godhead. When pranas are in harmony in the system, health is natural; when pranas are out of harmony, disease is possible. Pranayamas are procedures used to regulate the force and circulation of prana in the body, usually through regulation of the breathing rhythm.

Prarabdha Karma. Residual karmic patterns which are subject to restimulation and which can cause effects. These can be allowed to express and be exhausted, or they can be neutralized through prayer, meditation, certain yogic procedures, and the superior force of Self-Realization.

Rasa-Lila. The "eternal dance" taking place between the Lord of the universe and souls involved with creation.

Rasayana. *Rasa* can be translated to mean taste, juice, elixir or essence. The *ayana* part of the word means "pathway," "to circulate," or "to have a home or abode." In Ayur-

veda, rasayana treatment is a means of restoring the immune system so that body fluids circulate and find their
places in balanced harmony. Herbal compounds are usually
prescribed for rasayana therapy, and these preparations
are many and varied. For instance, one general-purpose
preparation contains raw sugar, clarified butter, Indian gall
nut, Indian gooseberry, dried catkins, Indian pennywort,
honey, nutgrass, white sandalwood, *evalyulus alsinaides*,
embrella, aloewood, licorice, cardamom, cinnamon, and
turmeric. Another includes *gumnema aurentiacum*, black
musale, butterfly pea, licorice, *vanda sphaerantus, indicus,*
heart-leaved moonseed, elephant creeper, and wild pepper.

Reincarnation. The process of being born into another flesh
body after departing one and resting in the astral sphere
for a duration. This doctrine is taught by enlightened
teachers, so there is no necessity of debating the concept.
One is drawn back to the material world so long as there
remains attachment to it, or if one has a duty to be performed. Some souls make their transition from the body
and continue to work out their spiritual freedom in subtle
astral or causal realms, before awakening in God, or experiencing complete transcendence.

Rishi. A seer, one who reveals Truth.

Sadhana. One's spiritual practices and involvement with processes designed to remove inner restrictions and result in
the experience of Self-realization. One can be involved
with such practices wherever he might be, whatever his
station in life. Transformation is an inner process.

Samadhi. When mental modifications no longer interfere with
soul awareness, samadhi is experienced. Samadhi is not an
unconscious trance state, but a state of clear awareness.
Initial samadhi states may be colored by feelings and perceptions. Higher samadhi states are unconditioned. Sahaja
samadhi is perfect soul awareness, even while using mind
and body in a natural way. Samadhi is a state of conscious-

ness; it is not knowledge, although one can acquire knowledge through samadhi if the intention is present.

Samkalpa. Determination, intention with mental conception, to cause something to come into existence through the exercise of pure will.

Samkhya. To enumerate, or number. Samkhya is the philosophical system which examines and explains the order of the universe by precisely describing all aspects of it. Samkhya philosophy is basic to the *Bhagavad Gita* and the *Yoga Sutras*.

Samsara. The "forever becomingness" of the world process. Unenlightened man is caught in the shifting currents of nature and experiences change whether he wants to or not. The ideal is to flow with change while being anchored in eternity.

Samyama. Perfect contemplation, as taught in the third section of the *Yoga Sutras*. Concentration, meditation, and identification with the object of concentration is perfect contemplation. In this way, if the intention is to know the reality of God, this can be known through experience. Through samyama the yogi acquires *siddhis*, soul abilities.

Sanatana Dharma. The eternal way of righteousness. Traced to pre-vedic times, it is said to be without origin, having its roots in Pure Consciousness, which is without beginning or end. The basic theme is that one should live in harmony with nature, attend to one's duty, and aspire to knowledge of God and Self-realization.

Sanyasin. A renunciate who has taken holy vows for the purpose of devoting all energies to Self-realization and, sometimes, world service.

Shakti. Cosmic creative energy which enlivens the worlds. Also the creative force in man which, when aroused, vitalizes the body and awakens kundalini.

Shaktipat. The infusion of shakti from guru to disciple. This can take place during initiation or anytime the disciple is receptive. Shakti can also begin to stir spontaneously when one is surrendered to God.

Shiva. The aspect of the Godhead which sends forth the worlds and then dissolves them, only to produce them again. Shiva is the patron deity of yogis. Shakti is Shiva's consort; between them the world process is made possible.

Siddha. A "perfected" being, a master of Yoga.

Siddhis. Powers of perfection, the capacities and abilities which unfold when inner restrictions are removed. The third section of the *Yoga Sutras* expounds in considerable detail on the subject of siddhis. Some of the abilities are: the power to be as small as an atom, to be as large as the universe, to be weightless, to see at a distance with remote vision, to do anything that is intended, and to be invincible.

Spiritual Eye. The third eye, the eye of intuition. The focus for this is in the space between the eyebrows. Here a yogi can enter the subtle realms or have mastery over space and time.

Spiritual Mind Treatment. A New Thought term referring to the procedure in which one becomes established in the awareness of God and then inwardly realizes that whatever he wants to see unfold is already accomplished in his mind and consciousness.

Sri Yukteswar. Disciple of Lahiri Mahasaya and guru of Paramahansa Yogananda. Born May 10, 1855, in Serampore, India, he entered mahasamadhi on March 9, 1936 at Puri.

Swami. A member of the ancient monastic order reorganized by Shankara in the Eighth Century. A swami is one who has renounced all ties and attachments and roams the world with God as his sole support.

Taoism. The old religion of China, said to have been inspired by the sage Lao Tsu, author of the *Tao Te Ching.* Emphasis is upon tranquillity, non-artificiality, simple enlightenment and non-acting (but letting).

Tattwa. The true or inner essence of a thing. The essence of the senses is the root of the senses in the mind. The essence of anything can be known through samyama, or perfect contemplation.

Transcendental Field. The unmanifest field of pure consciousness out of which all things emerge and into which they dissolve. One who experiences the Transcendental Field during meditation is resting at the very seat of power and creativity. Working from this level, all things in harmony with natural law are possible with minimum effort.

Turiya. The "fourth" state of consciousness transcending the three commonly experienced states of deep sleep, dream state, and ordinary waking state. Superconsciousness.

Upanishads. A collection of sacred texts which have origins in the oral teaching tradition. In centuries past in India, one would live with a guru in a retreat environment and "sit near" him to learn; hence the term, upanishad (upa-near; ni-down; sad-to sit). There are many upanishads, and Shankara wrote commentaries on several of them. These are called the Greater Upanishads because of their higher visibility. The Lesser Upanishads, which Shankara did not write commentaries on, contain advanced yogic instruction meant for the special few who were qualified to understand them. Among the Lesser Upanishads is the

Shandilya Upanishad, which was composed by one of Lahiri Mahasaya's ancestors. Kriya Yoga procedures are explained in it.

Vasana. Latent tendencies with roots in the unconscious. These tendencies, inclined in the direction of actualization, cause movement in the psyche, often resulting in experiences which are not anticipated. All latent tendencies with the potential to unduly influence should be neutralized, so Yoga teaches.

Veda. Veda refers to that which is self-revealed. The oldest known religious scripture in the world is the *Rig-Veda.* The Vedas contain the revelations of the ancient seers; the Upanishads offer philosophical explanation of them.

Vedanta. The summing up of the wisdom of the vedic tradition. The final wisdom is, "Supreme Consciousness is the cause, reality, and support of all that is."

Viveka. Discrimination between the changeless and the transitory. With discrimination, discernment, one sees without errors in perception.

Vyasa. A sage who is believed to have arranged many of the vedic works in their present form. Vyasa is probably the name used by many sages who worked on the project over the years.

Yama. The restraints recommended for one on the yogic path: harmlessness, truthfulness, non-stealing, regulation of all internal forces, and the absence of greed. The niyamas are the observances: internal and external cleanliness, serenity, intentional self-discipline, study of the nature of consciousness, and surrender of the ego-sense in order to realize the larger true nature, God. These guidelines apply to anyone on the spiritual path, regardless of time or place.

Yoga. To "yoke" or bring together all of the aspects of body, mind and personality so that Self-realization can be experienced. Various yogic systems include Hatha Yoga, "sun-moon" yoga, which involves body postures (*asanas*), *mudras* (life force control procedures) and pranayama; Bhakti Yoga, the way of love and devotion; Karma Yoga, the way of selfless service; Jnana Yoga, the way of intellectual discernment; and Raja Yoga, the way of meditation and contemplation. The basic text on Raja Yoga is the Yoga Sutras of Patanjali. Laya Yoga (use of sound), Kundalini Yoga (to awaken and work with the primal force in the body) and Kriya Yoga are a matter of emphasis, only.

Zen. The word is a transliteration of Ch'an, the Chinese for the Sanskrit word Dhyana, or contemplation. Dhyana became Ch'an in Chinese and Zen in Japanese. When Buddha attained enlightenment, the highest aspect of that experience could not be compared to anything known or unknown. During the lifetime of Buddha, religion in India had become ritualized. He pointed a way to spiritual freedom that transcended ritual. Some consider him to have been a "spiritual revolutionary" in this regard. It was shortly after this period of history that Shankara emerged to restate vedic principles in the light of knowledge. Buddhist influence moved through Tibet, to China and to Japan, as various sages traveled to spread the dharma, the way of righteousness.

Zoroastrianism. An ethical religious emphasis with roots in Persia (Iran).